HERE
TO
STAY

HERE TO STAY

Poetry and Prose from the Undocumented Diaspora

MARCELO HERNANDEZ CASTILLO, JANINE JOSEPH, ESTHER LIN

HARPER  PERENNIAL

NEW YORK • LONDON • TORONTO • SYDNEY • NEW DELHI • AUCKLAND

HARPER PERENNIAL

HERE TO STAY. Copyright © 2024 by Marcelo Hernandez Castillo, Janine Joseph, and Esther Lin. Page 229 is a continuation of this copyright page. Some material has been previously published in another format. All rights reserved. Printed in the United States of America. No part of this book may be used or reproduced in any manner whatsoever without written permission except in the case of brief quotations embodied in critical articles and reviews. For information, address HarperCollins Publishers, 195 Broadway, New York, NY 10007.

HarperCollins books may be purchased for educational, business, or sales promotional use. For information, please email the Special Markets Department at SPsales@harpercollins.com.

FIRST EDITION

Designed by Jen Overstreet

Library of Congress Cataloging-in-Publication Data has been applied for.

ISBN 978-0-06-322434-6 (pbk.)

24 25 26 27 28 LBC 5 4 3 2 1

For all of us—before, now, and to come.

I cannot separate my work from my undocumented identity.

—ALINE MELLO

CONTENTS

CONTENTS

CONTENTS

CONTENTS

UNDOCUPOETICS:
AN INTRODUCTION

A voice has emerged powerfully in the twenty-first century—that of the undocumented poet. It is a voice that had previously faced alienation of a curious order: a bureaucratic one. The Alien and Sedition Acts of 1798[1] and the Chinese Exclusion Act of 1882[2] in particular, form the beginnings of a labyrinth of systemic racism, wherein "aliens" could be arrested, imprisoned, and deported during wartime, and foreign workers could be recruited to the United States with the promise of work and prosperity in exchange for, in fact, the very opposite: the prohibition against employment and the government's iron right to deport and exile. What determined "citizen" from "alien" was volatile and depended often on perceived international enemies, fluctuating national quotas, and the interests of those in power. As journalist Jose Antonio Vargas writes in *Dear America: Notes of an Undocumented Citizen*, the signing of the Illegal Immigration Reform and Immigrant Responsibility Act (IIRAIRA) and the Antiterrorism and Effective Death Penalty Act in 1996 by the Clinton administration later "made it easier to criminalize and deport all immigrants, documented and undocumented, and made it harder for undocumented immigrants . . . to adjust our status and 'get legal.'"[3]

Though the racist motivations for passing those and scores of other similarly convoluted laws are well recorded, it is difficult to write creatively, let alone publish, about something as intangible as *status*. Until recently, the effort even seemed insurmountable. In January 2015, under the banner of the Undocupoets Campaign, friends and poets Marcelo Hernandez Castillo, Christopher Soto, and Javier Zamora circulated an open letter in protest of the discriminatory, immigration status–based practices of many poetry book contests, which required proof of legal residence or citizenship for submission or publication. This petition exposed the ways in which the literary community set up its very own border checkpoints, barring the undocumented poet entry. The directed campaign galvanized several landmark poetry book contests to revamp their exclusionary guidelines, marking the beginning of a significant shift in our literary landscape. Seeded in resistance and a disruption of the status quo, the undocumented poet rose into a changed field.

Here to Stay spotlights the poetry written by this extraordinary population. Our poets hail from various countries, cultures, religions, and educational histories. They create from within a spectrum of dis/abilities, live across various socioeconomic lines, and embody various gender and sexual identities. In our gathering, we issued a public call for poems written by poets who are currently or were formerly undocumented in the U.S. or who belong to a more complex "UNDOC+ Spectrum," a term theorized and coined by Erika Hirugami and Federico Cuatlacuatl, cofounders of the Undocu+Collective.[4] More specifically, we solicited work from a small selection of poets who come from mixed-status families and whose own lives and experiences are inextricably tied to their undocumented relatives, often their own parents and siblings. While Hirugami and Cuatlacuatl categorize citizen members of mixed-status families as within the adjacent "Undoc Diaspora," we want to collectively refer to the poets included here as our undocumented diaspora—a diaspora of our own within the larger poetry community.

Our inclusions demonstrate—crucially—how varied the undocumented poet's experience is. Among us, there are various statuses, including recipients of Deferred Action for Childhood Arrivals (DACA), holders of Temporary Protected Status (TPS), international students whose visas have expired, those who have crossed the Sonora Desert, formerly undocumented who have become newly naturalized citizens—to name a few. We all live with differing legalities, differing attainments of papers, and, therefore, differing predilections and attachments within our poems. Thus the feelings around one's own status—or of one's parents' status—are complex, often deeply ambivalent, and individual. Together, the fifty-three poets celebrated in this anthology prove there exists no monolithic undocumented narrative, no single undocumented experience, and no quintessential undocumented poem. *Here to Stay* seeks to challenge misconceptions of what it means to write as an undocumented person in twenty-first-century America and to offer a vision of the possibilities of our art.

We writers often like to talk about how we choose our own forms of art, how we choose according to how we negotiate our presence in the world. But equally important is the phenomenon that art chooses *us*; we recognize its potential for expression. We believe the undocumented poet has discovered poetry as a form that not only reflects their experience of the world but *reshapes* that experience. Moreover, we believe that the poet who has endured—to remix John Keats's theory of Negative Capability—the cruelties, uncertainties, mysteries, and doubts of the U.S. immigration system approaches our craft in newly imaginative, visionary ways. *Here to Stay* began with a theory realized over a series of yearslong conversations among the three of us—with Marcelo in California, Janine in the flyover country, and Esther in Seattle. We believe our poets can speak directly on how their lived experiences and art inform and influence each other. As three formerly undocumented poets, we understand how entrenched this experience's ramifications are; what dilemmas an undocumented individual bears on their own self, their family and community, in a nation founded on colonized land. How to survive? How to speak? And what do we say when our legal status is insufficient to capture the breadth of our wit, our innermost thoughts, our madcap lives? Who are best suited to theorize about the poetry of people from the undocumented diaspora but *us*? Who else but us are best equipped to shape the lens through which we are studied?

Why anyone chooses a poem as *the* vehicle of expression is a conversation for another book, but we can passionately theorize why *undocumented* people choose to write poems. In the case of those who have navigated reams of government forms to document undocumentedness, extending or outright flouting the "rules" offers a simple pleasure. Especially when "correctness" might interfere with force and expressiveness. For example, the breaking of a line: rather than stream across the page and run into the next line, as the sentences do in this paragraph, the poem's line races into an invisible white wall, and drops down to start all over again. Contributor Jan-Henry Gray observes, "Poems are like large rooms capacious enough to be filled with just about anything: fragments, bursts of language, and vivid observations. It's no wonder that poetry, with its profusion of broken lines, is home to so many of us."

To the undocumented poet, a poem's quietude, expanses of white space, moments of held breath, its desire for metaphor, its ability to disrupt, offer the relief of secrecy. Secrecy has been a powerful tool of survival for the undocumented. For better or worse, some of us have believed that to reveal our (or our family's) status to anyone, even a sympathetic friend, risks too much. We fear that "friend" may call Immigration and Customs Enforcement (ICE) and report to them our existence. We fear that they will love us so much that, in trying to find an answer we know doesn't exist, they will reveal our status to someone who doesn't love us at all. We fear that a slip of the tongue will leave a powerful scent that tracks the dogs straight to us. ICE would then arrest and deport us. Does it sound far-fetched? Maybe not. As of this writing, according to their website, ICE arrested 387,422 individuals between 2020 and 2023, many of whom were not the target of their search but happened to be in the way. Wrong place, wrong time.

A poem cannot protect a person without documents from arrest. But it is capable of a resonant whisper. As poets, we hope that risking this whisper is met with the gentle gift of a confidant who cares, empathizes, and is tender. Because it is often small, a poem might appear like a scrawled-on Post-it note found in a hallway. Or an elaborately folded message, handed across a classroom. In turn, the reader holds a distinct form of attention; experiences the intimacy of a secret, even forbidden, communiqué. Contributor Jane Kuo, who has published two novels, praises that aspect of poetry. She says, in more disquieting terms: This is "how I want the [reader] to feel, like a trespasser made privy to something intimate." By its nature, poetry lends itself well to art of the underground. To whisper, to express oneself via a disguise—artists in oppressive states rely on such tools. All this is achieved with tools available to almost everyone: pen, paper, and the mind.

We call the commonalities that arise in the poetry written by the undocumented diaspora as *undocupoetics*. Though the undocupoetic gesture is not new, we are naming it now. Inspired in part by the groundbreaking work of TC Tolbert and Trace Peterson in *Troubling the Line: Trans and Genderqueer Poetry and Poetics*, we invited contributors to introduce their work with a statement of poetics, or mini manifesto, describing the unique inner workings as they draft.

Undocupoetics is a portmanteau—of *undocumented*, the immigrant who settles in a country without approval from the state, and of *poetics*, a term that individualizes the way a poet uses language, imagery, structure, among other literary devices. That is, the elements that distinguish the poems written by the undocumented diaspora from the poems written by other Americans. We believe that these poems comprise their own distinct poetic, one that is identifiable, though not yet defined in the American literary tradition. From poet to poet, we also noticed echoes drawn from within and adjacent to the undocumented experience—in their tenderness toward elders, focus on flora and fauna, and even brief moments of humor, for example. Of course, not every poet is the same, and we hope this anthology exhibits the far-ranging curiosity and some of the complexities of each writer. Nevertheless, there are harmonies.

We have organized the anthology alphabetically according to the contributor's surname, allowing chance, rather than our ideas, to guide the reading experience. We did not wish to catalog our contributors according to the details of their status or relationships, in the way the U.S. government does. Indeed, we hope that you notice trends that only your own experience and sense of beauty can notice. We hope you notice the conversations that different poets seem to hold with each other. Perhaps you'll be as delighted as we were to notice that this anthology contains two poems starring dogs, written by two poets, presumably without each other's knowledge. (We have included in the back of the book a list of cross-references of trends that have stirred our own imagination and served as starting points for scholarly study.)

Chance like this was vital to our methodology. When we issued the open call for submissions of poetry from writers who are currently or formerly undocumented, we were pleasantly inundated with replies from self-selecting members of the undocumented diaspora. After choosing the poems to include, we sent each contributor individualized questions with the expectation that the contributor would craft their statement of poetics in response. Asking these questions thrilled us: we wanted to investigate what inspired their subject matters and their aesthetic choices; we wanted to reflect back what we observed of their poetics; we wanted to communicate closely with our community. In this way, we did not rely entirely by chance but acted (we hope) more like map-makers. We wished to curate, not dictate. The statements returned are more incisive, more sensitive, and more vibrant than anything we imagined. For the most part, we did not edit them—their own multiplicity would shine more brightly without our hands.

In their statements of poetics, contributors Saúl Hernández and féi her-nandez write on how surrealist language allows for them to metamorphose. Saúl Hernández notes, "We must transform ourselves into objects or creatures, defying logic—to write toward the realms of possibilities." One might even call this realm of possibility *home*. José Felipe Ozuna writes, "Poems have become a home for me, a place where I can say there are no borders, and it's true." While this imaginative work often seeks to correct the wrongs of an undocumented person's daily existence—and beyond—there is relief too. Wangeci Gitau writes of how their poems "speak to chasms, resolved or otherwise, ruptured while traversing the empire—and [their] attempt at creating a vessel for the diasporic angst that spills out." Aleyda Marisol Cervantes Gutierrez, Claudia Hernán-dez, Hermelinda Hernandez, and Patrycja Humienik speak earnestly of the safety and community that arise so powerfully perhaps *because* of the undocu-mented status. Humienik writes, "Borders lie—we belong not to nations but to each other and ourselves." Humanism over tribalism; community, rather than the forced division of families; poetry, rather than silence.

Many of the poems wrestle with the image the American public renders of the undocumented. In other words, who is the reader? Why is the reader read-ing this poem? What danger does the reader present? For Mico Astrid, to write is, in part, to educate their reader: "I hope to contribute truth to a collective memory that has long neglected to represent us with authenticity." Whereas Oswaldo Vargas anticipates hostility from the general world: "When social commentary and infrastructure tell me who I am and what I'm capable of due to my status, I say OK." In turn, his poems imagine possibilities wherein the speaker responds directly to the forces that circumscribe his life. There is ex-haustion, too, of the reader's expectations. Ayling Zulema Dominguez laments that the undocumented "must divulge in order to be seen." The exchange of private disclosure for public acknowledgment may feel exploitative for some contributors; it is cathartic for others. Leaning deliberately toward joy, Yosimar Reyes writes, "There is nothing beautiful about being undocumented, but if I must find something, it is that we found each other with our voices."

Far from a comprehensive survey, our anthology is a snapshot of how the undocupoetic appears to us during the years around 2024. Readers may expect subjects, emotions, histories, or perspectives that neither we nor our contributors mention adequately enough. We also expect for the undocupoetic to change swiftly and in direct response to its time. Laments Jesús I. Valles, "I am watching a genocide unfold from my palm, the architecture of this nation and our global present and domestic futures laid bare in Palestine. . . . I am experiencing such a tremendous distance from the person who wrote the poems you are reading in this anthology." We expect evolutions within our art as our diaspora grows in direct result of ongoing global conditions—famine, war, disease, natural disasters, poverty, and opportunity, to name a few—that force humans from their homelands and into legislative spaces. We write this, in fact, at a time shaped by a pandemic, significant climate change, and genocide. And as we brace for another election cycle in the United States, the "crisis of immigration" will certainly regain currency on the national stage and in public imagination.

Likewise, change will surely occur as the undocupoetic continues to intersect with other discourses, theories, and schools of thoughts. A good forecast of this change is glimpsed in Wo Chan's luminous meditation on the body and the transformative, revolutionary capabilities of drag, as well as Tobi Kassim's profound discussion of borders, binaries, fugitivity, and DACA. And we expect the undocupoetic to change if only because poetry demands change. Poetry, as with all art, wishes to disrupt itself. Therefore, such things are difficult to predict, but we hope that the endeavor of this anthology legitimizes a serious study of our work. In the literary landscape, we are here to stay.

On a final note, we wish to celebrate this community's courage in sharing their poetry and prose. It is a distinct quandary of the undocumented diaspora that not all of us are comfortable or in a position to reveal our own or our family's status. As editors, we are grateful. As fellow members of the undocumented diaspora, we are proud.

Here is a new field of poetry, of study, of play, and of cultivation. Whoever you are, we invite you in—and through.

In solidarity,

Marcelo Hernandez Castillo, Janine Joseph, Esther Lin
Undocupoets co-organizers

An undocumented person is a person who has settled in the United States without explicit sanction from the government. These include students and tourists whose visas have expired, refugees traversing the U.S.-Mexican border, and refugees who have been removed from Temporary Protected Status due to shifts in U.S. policy. At the time of this writing, there is no serious attempt by the federal government to assist this estimated population of eleven million undocumented immigrants. And those affected by this lapse in federal policy are not only the eleven million but the communities around them: families and friends who risk the danger of loved ones who might be deported.

A. A. ASHER

When I was able to return to my home country after being away for sixteen years, I noticed the strange howling of dogs one night. The time difference made it difficult to sleep, but I was often up anyway thinking of whether I could return to America, literally and figuratively, which is now my new home. The lines for the poem "Hope" formed every evening as I wondered whether the dogs were caged or free to roam and as I thought of my own relationship with my childhood family dog called Hope. At the long line of the immigration counter that bordered my reentry to the U.S. I began to look through the lines of bodies entering through customs for global citizens, the U.S. citizens, the international visitors, and wondered where I truly fit. The stereotypical identity of an undocumented person living in America is often not Black. If you're Black you're often associated with being a refugee—there must have been a reason for you to have left your country, one that is urgent and one that requires a pardon. In "Venus, a Dollar," I remember Sara Baartman, a South African woman who was displayed as part of a freak show of Africans in Europe. I want to call attention to what one is required to see and what is omitted. I want to consider language and labels as a form of oppression.

Venus, a Dollar

—Portsmouth, NH

America is a museum
and Venus is on display
for a dollar, you can touch
the ===== of a ==== woman
who came straight from the =====
of Africa. They know how to ====
they carry ===== or =====
in their wombs see how round

       Audience(in unison and excitement): wow

we want to preserve the way
we show this =====
so please refrain from using
a ===== when capturing her =====
don't go too close to the ====
at times she gets =========
but we have methods of security
to keep everyone safe

Dog Poem

Hope and I ate
from the same plate

Fufu and soup.
I offered Hope bones

& Hope sat at my feet.
He was a big brown dog.

Here, we don't keep
dogs on leashes.

They know where to roam,
how to return

to the smell
of their owners,

how to bark
the gates open.

Hope dies
and the replacement

dog receives his name.
This is when my trauma begins.

I am looking for Hope
in every dog. When I return

HERE TO STAY

to the city where Hope is killed
by a taxi driver,
I hear my neighbor's dogs.

They don't see
each other,

only sunrise
and sunset.

When thieves are absent,
the darkness echoes

an orchestra of howls
which wakes the dying

crows who have started
to eat themselves. No one

is innocent in this country.
When the dog show

ends, I slip into the sheets,
& imagine the dogs

Stretch their front paws
& smell Bougainvillea, sprouting.

MICO ASTRID

Through my work, I commit myself to memory as an act of revolt. To be an immigrant in America is often a continuous attempt to survive where you are not wanted and not welcome—as communicated through legislation, through denial of rights, through direct and indirect harm. In a world where key facets of marginalized peoples' identities and rights are publicly debated and rescinded, I hope to contribute truth to a collective memory that has long neglected to represent us with authenticity. For people to understand injustice, they must be able to see what is happening. For people to see what is happening, they must be able to see us.

In this way, writing about my lived experience is an invitation for readers to expand their own memory, so that we may be able to understand each other amidst all our nuanced grief and struggle. Often, my work focuses on arranging symptomatically dissonant language reclaimed from other sources—from government documents to personal conversations—in order to illustrate the stark realities endured by people living in harsh diaspora. With this dissonance, I hope to invite readers to ask, *Why is it like this?* and to someday arrive at an answer that propels us collectively closer, and forward.

In the Corner of a Small World

empty apartment sunlight
trash bins nestled in young grass
a treehouse in a child-sized tree
summer is a dream i had
before all of them filled with blood

my mother visited in october
she fell and hit her head and
didn't tell me
emergency room secret
her laugh is hollow like always in her stories that are hollow like always
hollow and light

once
in a borrowed bed she sang to me "
just face the rising sun and you'll see hope there's no need to run"
"lift up your hands to"
"god"
"and he will give"
"you"
"rest
"

we curled up like burning twigs—quick and dry and made to burn

Some Responses

Well, there must be another way

Wow, I never would have guessed

What is that even like?

It's not your fault your parents brought you here

19 years? Why so long?

God, that sounds terrible

It's not like you're from the Philippines at all anymore

That's like when I had to apply for dual citizenship

I'm sure there's something you can do

We need a better way for smart people like you

Can't you just join the military?

Do you even have anywhere to go if you were deported?

I know, yeah, the government is soo hard to work with

You've never traveled outside of the country? That's so sad

You're still doing that?

HERE TO STAY

Well, have you tried applying for citizenship?

Right, but we also have to keep dangerous people out

Can you get your green card already so we can travel?

Why haven't you married a citizen yet? Seems easy

I didn't realize you're Hispanic

Have you considered this? I found it on Google

Well, I don't think they'll deport you

I'm pretty sure you can still vote

Well, you aren't like the rest of them

You're lucky to be here at all

LAUREN CAMP

I began writing the poems of *One Hundred Hungers* because I wanted to understand my father's childhood in Iraq. I wasn't writing for anyone else. I was simply investigating a closed space, a history that had been walled off to me. Since he wouldn't speak about why the family left, wouldn't answer questions about his early past, I began with what I could access: food, faith, and family.

From all the times we'd gathered at my grandparents' home, I knew the many flavors and spices, the aura of the language and the familiar interactions.

My father never said the family "fled." He spoke only about arriving. Only about starting a new life. Over and over, I brought my father's mysterious culture to the page as sound or energy. Through research, I came to learn of the religious persecution his family had faced. I began to formulate a clear understanding of why they chose to take refuge elsewhere, unmoored from everything they knew about themselves.

My father was granted his naturalization certificate nearly six years after stepping foot on US soil in 1950. What parts were difficult? What wasn't? I write often about emptiness, standing on both sides of it and praising or being disquieted by it. By imagining variations of the truth and talking directly into the quiet spaces, I was able to unlock the project. Absence and silence were weighted, but utterance was agency. On the page, I had the chance to query what seemed missing.

One Hunger Could Eat Every Other

We sit at the long table. My grandfather speaks until the entire alphabet exists in the palm of my hand. I swallow but can't discern a word.

Outside, branches stand, lit from within.

The last reason and consolation: the song of our fathers.

In this house, our lips envelop the bread, the egg yolk and honey, the braid of the yeast, our lamentations. Men are smoking, unhurried. Women leave the room and return with gray hair.

We sit across from whoever appears, aunts from Toronto, Tel Aviv, London, South Africa. Distant cousins and uncles and business partners. We remember their names, their bruised pickled syllables. We'll see them again.

> *Here is my grandmother. She stayed in the kitchen, cooked chicken for dinner. Onto plates, rice with raisins. Into bowls, string beans and okra. She brings out the food, blessing her sons without speaking. My grandmother, toothless.*

The truth lives in my grandmother's *kitchri*, the butter-gush and red-cheeked lentil. In the wide white pans and platters.

For weeks and years we return, seizing all beet and fig, skin and bone, eating slabs and glands with our fingers, watching invisible gazelle, hearing owl. This goes on and on. My uncles argue. Each defense is as close as they come to caress.

> *One uncle pulls at his jowls. Another pulls out his money—all C-notes. He makes sure we see as he counts, forward and back. My father sighs from his chair in the room with tall windows. His eyelashes crowd together, curve down. He once told me—The dust gets trapped in our eyes. My lashes let me go out in the world.*

We eat for years and years. We eat like beggars. We eat to the bones and the edges of our plates. We eat the road they took to get here, the many myths they left behind. We grab with our hands, our mouths still full. We eat until the tablecloth is stained with conversation, and the severed tongue of a cow, beet-grief, the village air.

Watch the elderly aunt—Victoria, with her tired red shawl and box of old cakes. Everyone talks without punctuation, and the room is a river of sound down the long cloth with its flashes of garnet.

We eat each clutch of sweet, salt, fat, plight. After many bowls and forks. Until gorged, until demolished. What is lost is more succulent than what was gained. We eat until the table is again table, a collection of plates with small pearls of leftover fat.

In the kitchen sink, dishes pile up with utensils. Remaining grease and grains of rice embellish warm rivulets of water.

At the back door at dusk behind boxes and screen, a black cat with a broken tail is entangled in the yellow-eyed daisies. My aunt pours him some milk, her fingers tired and bent. A train bleats as it rolls past. The cat flares, then gorges on liquid. Both sounds spill out from the dark, side by side.

The thick line of life is all hunger. We eat as the sky recedes to countless diaphanous layers. We eat as logic, loyal. Knowing it will end.

Either we are full—or tired of the howl.

After midnight, we drive home, over the bridge, past the thick wheat and sugar smearing the Bronx, past every reference, through the confident dark.

Pause Hawk Cloud Enter

The soup cooks for an hour while vultures and buzzards pluck the market.
My father wipes his forehead with a white cloth.

Once, each day began with *khubz* and *samoon*
flat and hot from the griddle, and sips of *sharbat* with sandalwood petals.

Those beside the river were not aware of other places. No one knew
how long the water ran, ran, trying to get where it had never been.

My father hears nothing and nothing becomes the gate
he walks through. There is nothing
but what has been erased.

Listen to the clumsy way he watches the pigeons,
and his laugh when they lift a few streets off.

It takes a whole life to make a man, but there was a day
he raised his overstuffed suitcase, the day he was sent for,

the day the desert left its pungency. That day
denied him one future and brought him the trampled ground of another.

My father dines on his languages: garlic and lemon. On barley and river.
There is hunger and hunger lined up on his spoon.
Candied apricot, yogurt, his sixth birthday, his seventh.

Take the pot from the flame.

I was born on ashes. Cotton and silk left in basements,
on old candelabras and alleys. On someone else's recent past. On clotted sky.

How do you live in silence? You talk to absence.

You eat, tasting the steam. The ingredients vary.
You smash the door.
You erase and erase until what you've kept is transparent.

You watch the earth in the window, your body browning.

WO CHAN

A poem is a window, a mirror, or a door. It can be all three at once; it can be one at a time. A poem can be a window in one decade, a mirror today, and a door tomorrow. Brief lyrics glimpse for us the secrets of another life; reading an epic, you slowly realize the struggle described in the text is your own.

To have a body is to be a window, mirror, and door, all at once and one to all.

Teaching poetry, you say: "Look at the body of the text, the shape the poem makes sitting on the page." We stare at this shape, the pool of letters anchored in vast beige, because there is knowledge to be appreciated, because this shape was set with intention and deep feeling. Another way to say it—because it is beautiful.

We want this same beauty for our own form, to be able to delight in our own reflection, crafted with a precise intention as language, yearning and play-ful. And dearly, we want to claim this beauty (the language, the craft) stitch by stitch, letter by letter as our own. This is knowledge.

Put another way, poetry is language fantasy, a wish made into expression, the same way that drag is the fantasy of the body. Not just what is possible, but against that which is forbidden. A poem transforms paper into hope; drag transforms the body into great beauty and pride, despite social and political op-pression. Both require massive effort. Both can be—not just expressions—but visceral assertions for societal transformation. And both declare: "My name is _____, and I have something to say."

This is the knowledge we share.

performing miss america at bushwig 2018, then chilling

breathe . . . some reddish dolphins (these bare feet busted),
tore through my capezios, unmoisturized, they join
your pilgrim black boot—oh my mammal . . .
the wide weekend's long disclosure of drugs drawn

precious, depressed, high-function high anxious: 2018
gifts us fed dossiers on our stupendous thumbs-down needs.
you need therapy. i need money. we ditch our brains
unable to shred the fog of futures where civics, passion,

paycheck, and pleasure meet. two hours ago, we ran late through slashing
rain on Smith, tumbling you, your sister, (family) in the uber xl backseat,
helped me paste a glittering red AMERICA on my toilet paper sash.

we made it. early at bushwig, barely attended, i exploded the bouquet,
rolled nakedly on stage. i didn't expect to make 14 dollars cash,
crumpled. i took mushrooms as planned. time unclenched. i found you! sipping rosé

backbar, i was so happy. joy was flapping its wings in the dustbath!
you said i didn't seem different but by then i could no longer bear violence,
however simulated. i wanted only to see soft things: your empath
friend, Our Lady of Paradise, gives guided meditations, undoing some violence
in synchrony, she sings under the megawatts of her holographic leotard:
new songs about her gender dysphoria.
my smile pancakes beyond the edges of my cuisinart
face "she's so greeeaaaat" i say stretching like an accordion.

but, how useful are words now? by then i had lost the white pearls
glued on my décolleté—they dropped far like seeds from a seagull's asshole.
thinking about a feeling is like photocopying a feeling. that scanning light is safe.
i brag my brain is fearless, yet i wear my heart smeared across my face.
waiting for the all-gender bathrooms with you, i just wanted to sit and melt
like kerrygold into your fur coat. you said it was real. i knew that. i felt it.

"People Like You More Than You Know"

no wrong falls dirt on the ass planted
pasta sauce squat kinky mid broadway
starching scritch-scratched zuchettes yodel
PLENTITUDE in their trader joyful
cooler bag, strapped & streetpicked blue.

oh she thinks it is autumn in her
unstoned tracksuit she commutes long distances
dinner with her analyst flatbush friend
a butternut dildo squash, she wears vertical houndstooth
slices vertical a kirakira plus zuchh

this conversation on mothers
is not going well freewheeling they do not
heal fast enough she doesn't call she's hung up
on some if not oh definitely the same
childhood she misses the thickness she admits

life
clenching is her own genius so angry it snags
the oilslicked cradle of fish unblinking
casts a shade of blue tyvek flags
laid lidding the ground zero site of all feelings

begs for belief
the night softens its eyes on the unionized forest
the water unbraids itself, clear and limp
i love my neoclassical marbled eye rounds
i love this body made of bones, aluminium, the rubber of old doorstops

HERE TO STAY

i have wanted to not exist
and i have wanted to be her
i have wanted some epic use for my excellent enjambed body
i want the water to soften on the unionized forest
i want the clear night to limp into my eyes

Special Special

    jump into rob's arms koala   embrace
the expressions of wonderloaf   looks like blankness
    makes me think they are liars.   january's baby spinach
begins to yellow a small hole. i toss, unstomach
    the trashbin, sing thank you lanky hanger, thanks old hat. everyone is listening.
i asked "what's a fake poem?" and "how do I make money?"
    my shirt white with bedbug powder antagonistically
is diatomic earth   smith street's snowplow spittles
    salt on the ground flurries a fantastic, classic burlesque
makes me want to give chase and tussle
    french fries in its wake   Feed the Multitudes
with what i say   how i say   me, i say   forever?

    and, overnight, philadelphia in the sight mirror   i undress
myself cream and crest, twist in this stiff saddle, my quadriceps
    pinkening, a decision to eat landmeat again, share
love poetry, the rogue footage of my strawberry
ass arched high as cathedral glass.   what is your biggest dream,
what is it? i asked every first date, what it is should embarrass you.
why did i, twenty-five, bully these men who dreamed their purebred frenchies,
winter glazing on american territories, the unwilting rooftop nursery—?
I too wanted the hard, sustainable property where my brief name stretches
to rim the acreage of this good future.   Do we get to live again? (the prodigy,
my neighbor, violin expert, a slam poet, the model in corset, cartwheeler, modern
dancer, designer, someone genius, someone kind, someone with no needs,
savvy, an activist, a healer, my own mother, a double citizen, three deportees,
the figure in the fisheye unvanishing, rounds the corner—)
    all the goodness i've been mistaken for

LAUREL CHEN

I used to think my writing was a portal—a means of imagining, of world building and possibility. I now see my writing as, in the words of Fargo Nissim Tbakhi, "more than healing, witness, catharsis, community, imagining otherwise." My poetics are the product of my ESL brain long forced to twist language into belief, making meaning from sound. A teacher of mine, Myung Mi Kim, once taught me to look at the poem as a continuum—gradations where language is constantly occurring, because language is not a given. Nearly every instance of language in my life where there is authority has been derived from the state and its many abuses of power. I am clear that my poems will not tear down prison walls, shut down weapons manufacturers, or bring back loved ones from premature death. Instead, I write, to borrow from Ruth Wilson Gilmore, because freedom is a place: a location, a geography, an assemblage of people and our commitments to each other. Freedom is a place—may every poem I write be evidence that we are nearing it.

Greensickness

After Gwendolyn Brooks

My wild grief didn't know where to end.
Everywhere I looked: a field alive and unburied.
Whole swaths of green swallowed the light.
All around me, the field was growing. I grew out
My hair in every direction. Let the sun freckle my face.
Even in the greenest depths, I crouched
Toward the light. That summer, everything grew
So alive and so alone. A world hushed in green.
Wildest grief grew inside out.

I crawled to the field's edge, bruises blooming
In every crevice of my palms.
I didn't know I'd reached a shoreline till I felt it
There: A salt wind lifted
The hair from my neck.
At the edge of every green lies an ocean.
When I saw that blue, I knew then:
This world will end.

Grief is not the only geography I know.
Every wound closes. Repair comes with sweetness,
Come spring. Every empire will fall:
I must believe this. I felt it
Somewhere in the field: my ancestors
Murmuring *Go home, go home—soon, soon.*
No country wants me back anymore and I'm okay.

If grief is love with nowhere to go, then
Oh, I've loved so immensely.

HERE TO STAY

That summer, everything I touched
Was green. All bruises will fade
From green and blue to skin.
Let me grow through this green
And not drown in it.
Let me be lawless and beloved,
Ungovernable and unafraid.
Let me be brave enough to live here.
Let me be precise in my actions.
Let me feel hurt.
I know I can heal.
Let me try again—again and again.

Judicial

Aliens do not fall from the sky, we fail
    From it. Point upward & say yes. This is where

We first alighted. This is how we molded
    A landscape from sorrow. Even after all

These years, what I really want isn't papers.
    I know already about the miracle

Of flight. I am waiting for you to give me wings.
    I learned to count my age in years past

The expiry date. My memory, already fading
    Into a shoreline that vanishes before I even

Reach it. The cost of immigration is forgetting
    The cost of immigration. I begin to break

in a new tongue the same pace I learn how to leave
    my loved ones behind. Sometimes, I tilt

My skull skyward. Let my mouth run with English.
    Please. I am trying to remember. Believe me.

Sanctuary

When I hear my mother's voice losing its honey, my heart beats
    So quickly it shakes. My rib cage a sudden burst

    Of bees. Immigration without homegoing is just
An insect frenzy. We drained the ocean of salt so now

We come for sweet. Immigration: a syrup sickness.
    Immigration: a swarming mass scattered across amber waves

    Of pain. Look: I come from a people leaving.
Look: they drew a line through the water & the hours grew

Between us. Listen: don't you hear my migrant heart
    Humming from this side of the earth?

    Someday, I imagine my mother will be singing.
    There is a world where I awaken

    Under another chest or a new name
        inheriting nothing but relief.

    If I am alive, I am still on my way.
    I know this. We are humming
        The whole way home.

AYLING ZULEMA DOMINGUEZ

Born to a mixed-status family and a body that "Western" history deemed a site of colonization, yearning was my first alphabet and diasporic poetics my first language. In the American education system, we are taught to perceive colonialism as a thing of the past, when every day I would go home to a family presently deeply affected by the U.S.-Mexico border: hard proof of ongoing colonial occupation and segregation. I began writing stories because my ears alone were an insufficient receptacle for the ancestral songs and immigrant lyrics I was bestowed at the dinner table. I quickly learned the blank page is not always the most welcoming space for writers of lineages impacted by colonial violence; an insinuation that we must divulge in order to be seen, that our pages are blank to begin with and it is up to us to fill them, when really, we are surrounded by the voices who came before us and have cenotes of ancestral memory to remember and recount from. My writing is bodily because I know we house the necessary imaginations for liberation within us. My writing takes dirt by the handful, recites oceansong, threatens border regimes, and builds ladders to freer skies. I want us to remember an interconnectedness and collective care beyond current societal constraints, and to take up all the space and breath on the page and with our voices in order to arrive there.

Flood Waters

I   grew   asthma   in   the   womb
because   even   then I   wanted closeness.
I wanted   your   heart   to   seep   into me.

Instead   I   choked   on   blood and   bile   and   water.
It   entered   my lungs   the way   a child   throws   a rock across
the pond,   wanting it   to skip   and it

sinks. It happens when
a baby is stressed—a gasp, a
gulp.

My   first   dialogue with   desire,
my   first interface   with longing, left me
lamentable   lungs   and   a measly body
that   associated   love   with
submersion.

This   engulfed   body   has   no   room   for grudges,
I promise.   Contrary   to   poetic tendency, I don't have   my
grievances
numbered   and   listed.   I   just   have
this   inland   sea.   Yearning freezes   it over each   season
and   the   marine   life   below   are
preserved   in   numbness.

Our   homelands   and   lineages   were
introduced   to   the   invasive   species   of
brutality   and conquest, handed to   us   so that we   may do the work of
destroying ourselves   for   those   who envision a horizon without
us.   That   is   why   tomorrow already
feels   underwater.

I   hope that   I   might   find   you   in
the   flood.

GRECIA HUESCA DOMINGUEZ

When I immigrated to New York from Veracruz, Mexico, I was old enough to remember the life I was leaving behind. But with time, my memories became murky. About sixteen years later, I began to write down my memories of those ten years after I realized something I had held as true was a dream instead. Initially, a panic washed over me as I questioned that memory. My good memory had helped me through school, and at work people often praised my ability to recall small, important details. To have my memory trick me felt like a betrayal. I decided to conserve my memories in poems because poetry allowed me to focus on their emotional truth.

In my writing, I am selfish—I write for myself first and everyone else second. When I could no longer count on the accuracy of my memory, I crafted each poem to exist only for me. I create the world of a poem not only through my eyes but for my eyes. My poetry eventually progressed past writing only about those first ten years, especially once I started sharing my work and it found its way to other undocumented people. I am still surprised that I write about my small life and that the power of poetry takes over and readers can give life to each poem well beyond the page.

Christmas Eve in San Diego After Crossing the Border

We told her we had already converted our pesos to dollars. She told us to walk all the way down the rolling hill and we'd find the Burger King. We were instructed not to talk to anyone but the cashier, if the cashier didn't speak Spanish we were to order using our fingers. We learned a new skill and walked back to the house with food none of us craved. It had been nice being out for a bit. To get a break from the smell of mucus coming from the room that housed the bedridden husband attached to an oxygen tank. The lady said when he fell ill, she started taking in people to make money and that it was nice to have company on Christmas Eve. That night we all sat in her living room and we told stories of what we would be doing if we were with our families. Such a quiet night. There was no music or tamales or people dropping by the house to say hello and drink a rompope with us like every other Christmas Eve. There were only French fries and the smell of mucus.

All the Divorced Mexican Women I Meet Are Happy

In Veracruz, my grandmother, the impeccable widow, sits beneath the coolness of the mango tree and mourns my grandfather as if he just died the day before. She tells me she's happy my father found a new woman—now he has someone to take care of him.

At the beach, I stare out past the horizon as one woman tells me she can let her wild laugh surge now that she is divorced. Another might have wished her ex-husband dead but settles for not having to hear his opinion about how she spends her money anymore. A family friend shows me the spot where she and her sister go to drink coffee. They sit and face the sea breeze with a hot cup of coffee in their hands, plenty of gossip on their lips, and their feet submerged in the warm sand. We sit there and drink coffee too.

She tells me I did the right thing and moved on with my life. She tells me about men and the things they do to wives. She tells me the things her own father did to her mother and the things my grandfathers did to my grandmothers.

Back in the US, my mother leaves New York and moves to the South with her dog. She sends me video after video of the dog playing in the surf, my mother laughing in the background as the dog fights each ebbing wave. Here at home, I sit with the story women have always known about men, a story of heartbreak and suffering that often doesn't end until the man is dead.

How beautiful it is that we found our way out in life! How joyous it is that we get to make our own joy and feed our own hunger.

JUAN RODRIGUEZ DOMINGUEZ

This poem is a segment of a project I worked on about an unreliable narrator confined by different vectors of their identity. In this poem, they grapple with the fact that they are an immigrant who is in a constant state of mourning. As many others have experienced at some point, the narrator is trying to make sense out of a particular change that occurred in their life, recreating the images they saw in the past, but frustrated with their inability to grasp the incident in its entirety due to the malleable nature of memory. The narrator never details the physical parts of the individual they miss. The narrator only mentions their person's gender, which creates ambiguity. Who is this individual that does not have a proper eulogy? The only clues one has come from the museum, which is both subject to fabrication and incomplete. The narrator feels confinement, which is where the structure of the poem comes into play. The poem is in a box, a case per se, which can also represent a makeshift casket. There are columns in the poem, which function as a contrapuntal, but their purpose is also to create a sense of incongruence and anxiety. The more one writes, the more divisions they encounter, and the less space they have to process and capture what's haunting them. I guess the idea I wanted to get across with the narrator is that certain poems, like many things in life, will always be incomplete.

Case # XXXX

Utilizing the bones and feathers of an owl,
he constructed a museum inside his [father's] backpack,
a large raggedy red bag with a sundry of stitches
that once gathered a constellation of dimmed stars
from across countless unmapped villages.
Incandescent spheres that collapsed
and coalesced into the soil that became the burial ground
of forgotten gods and languages
who abided by the second law of thermodynamics.
Something about closure
propels us towards madness. An inconsumable body
of water one dreads, but still thirst over. A desire for touch
that can be traced like a cicatrice, a tributary
of memories that conceive speech. An oil painting
that will never dry, and the rugged hands
that will never clench the spines of disassembling visions.
He was an insatiable and repenting bastard.
He knew his museum would one day crumble,
but he built it anyway, believing it would ease
the silence of [decay].
          He curated three exhibits.
The first was a replica of a modest shrine
consisting of a carved statue,
A ceramic bowl with crumbs of bread,
and unscented candles.
The second was a poorly spackled wall
that displayed slabs of torn muscle, cartilage, sinew,
and coagulated blood.
The third was a brick passage
that contained a list of phone numbers,
a photograph of a young boy, and a folder
of half-written letters
addressing someone in [North Carolina].

He spoke of a fourth installation,
but before he finished
arranging the galleries of poppies
and ocotillos, monarchs
scavenged the clavicles
of his cardboard corridors.
It's been fifteen years since then;
your left hand is holding a scapular,
your right hand is holding
a fountain pen
you're attempting to unearth
the lacuna of his final thoughts,
but you've never been able to,
and each venture to encroach
the territory of that [winter] day
instead revises you
and leaves you with fewer words
to properly mourn a man
who was not granted rites
or eulogies, a man whose face
you can no longer remember.
Hours veer toward [dusk]
and you're not sure if the God
you envision is the one he followed,
the reason the cost of admission
for his museum was a marigold
and a flask of mezcal,
or if anyone will believe you
when the winds already refused
to testify his existence.

KEVIN SERRANO ECHEVARRÍA

I am undocumented by only a few miles—the city of my birth landing square on the U.S.-Mexico border. And yet those few miles have been stretched into twenty-seven years and over two thousand miles away from that dotted line I failed to cross before being born. It's a sick joke to be a Mexican who grew up in Wisconsin. And a sick joke to grow up queer in a small town.

My poetry is an attempt to stretch borders and definitions to where I am and who I am. I want to merge these artifacts of nationality, masculinity, and sanity with their counterparts and create something whole from them—something that denies distinction between personal narratives, which, in my opinion, is the goal of all poetry. When I first wrote this poem, I intended to give it a body that can represent its essence in corporeal form. But by doing this, it felt inauthentic to the contradictory and ineffable experience of undocumentedness. The meaning lies, if anywhere, someplace in the middle. And so, I have two opposing bodies and let the meaning fall somewhere in between. Just as we deviants (of gender or nationality or of all imposed borders) find our bodies—material or immaterial—somewhere in between.

Img. 1

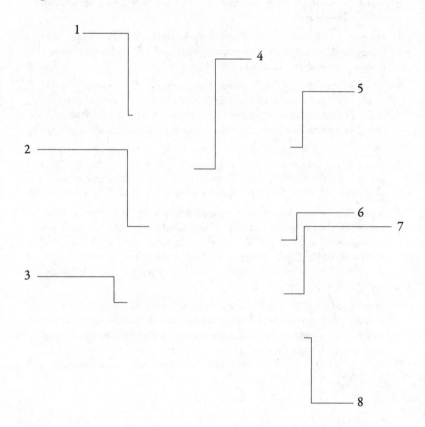

1- There are old words that echo / from the beak of the hummingbird / tales and names inhabited / only in the tip of my tongue / and fluttering out of my mouth / in the shower or on the bus / They are cousin / they are birthday cakes / they are government letters forged / across national boundaries / They're the ashes of could've beens / from across the edge of the horizon / enough to withstand a thousand sleepless evenings / enough to pull the Sun across the sky

2- My great-grandfather lives / on the yellow blades / strewn across the dirt/ I collect in my rosy palms / and stop short / of driving them across my throat / to feel his bronzy fingers / gather up my vocal chords / and tell the stories / I've only heard in passing

3- Let me / wipe away this / painted face / and wring out these / semen-stained blood cells / to be planted in the soil / two thousand miles across / to be swallowed up / by the roots of the cempasúchil / to become the shame / of two thousand forebearers

4- His name was stained / on the fabric of my boxerbriefs / when mamá tried to bleach it out / with lime juice before trying to scratch it off / with Lee press-ons / unaware that each acrylic scrape / drove him in deeper

5- Father, what is family? / Could I still be yours / half a hemisphere away? / Could I still / carry your name / in another man's tongue? / Could I keep your memory / trapped under a child-lock / and watch it glow / in the amber-colored plastic? / Could I keep your face / beneath mother's stolen cosmetics? / Father, what is a faggot?

6- Kevin. Kevin. It's time. / I know it's not the weight of the heavens / that keep you in bed / but how easy / a hell is to carry in your chest / Come sit on the snowpile / and see the Sun / beating like a heart in the sky

7- A child will be sprawled / on the Chicago pavement / on the Milwaukee snowbanks / on the California dusthills / Blood straight from the heart / will rain on the Sonora / seep into the Great Lakes / and circulate through the banks and rivers / of every red-stained state / and Podunk-town / fed by muddy palms / But for now / his father holds / his newborn's heart / and promises to be a better man / than he knows he will be

8- A thirteen-year-old is killed by the police / as I celebrate ten years / of being stranded on the dotted line / My body becomes / a long-healed scar on the earth / moving ever northward / as those around me drop off / and become hills and sand dunes / painting the ground / the warm, orange glow / of the sunsets / so I lay down beside them / and wonder if we'll ever come back / as hummingbirds

JOSÉ FELIPE OZUNA

I left Mexico and crossed the border into the U.S. when I was four years old. I ask my mother to tell me the story again and again because I'm always forgetting. When I was younger, terrified of forgetting, I would write down phrases I heard, ask my family about what they said hours ago. I think in a way those were my first poems.

Writing is a way for me to remember and archive in a way that feels emotionally true. The reshaping of reality that happens in my poems isn't about the need to hide, but the need for something else, something better, than what actually happens. Poems are attempts to regain whatever was lost when I left Mexico, to make meaning out of unjust deaths, to attempt a different understanding of a relationship.

Every poem I write is an undocumented poem because every day I'm an undocumented immigrant. Today I learned that the Biden administration is willing to increase border security and deportations in order to get Republican support for a bill investing billions in military aid. Is there anything more indicative of how disposable we are as immigrants? How we are used as a bargaining chip? Can you blame my speaker for wanting _____?

Poetry is a place where I don't have to make concessions. I can write a poem with horses, with no line breaks, with dragons, with children catching stones in their mouths. Poems have become a home for me, a place where I can say there are no borders, and it's true.

Elegy for the Ones Who Didn't Make It

> On June 27, San Antonio police and Homeland Security investigators found
> 64 migrants, some inside the truck, in the sweltering Texas heat and others in
> its vicinity ... Forty-eight of them died at the scene and 16 others were trans-
> ported to hospitals. Five of those 16 people died at the hospital.
> —NBC News

Let me give you a different ending.
Where the truck's doors open

and you all come spilling out
and breathing. Skin like oak,

every wrinkle holding a life's worth of sun.
Outside, there's a train waiting to take you—

to the new life you came to build,
though you'll wonder if you'll ever call it home.

And you'll make a list of reasons to uncross the border:
Mamá's tortillas, the soft heat, tomatoes and mangos so ripe

and flush with color they look like they were pulled
from every sunset that's ever grazed the horizon.

Back home the wind swayed you while you slept
in hammocks. Back home even the birds sang your name.

Sometimes you'll ask the creases in your palms
why you even came. Days are marked with snow,

hard stares at your spine, the silence
when you enter a room filled with language

you cannot fit your lips around.
But here—la familia! Who'll hug you

and won't let go, hands squeezing tight
against backs they thought were lost.

I want to believe that's enough.
It might have to be.

When it's time, we'll break down every border.
Run the train through the wall. Leave a hole wide enough

for our gente to come in droves. Black hair blowing through sunroofs
past the border agents we have _____. Streets lined with politicians

we have _____. It is violent. It is beautiful. In this ending,
we don't forget about you. You're not a headline buried among many.

In this ending, I don't have to look up how many of you died
before I write this. You are not dead.

I don't write this.

Is There Anything as Still as Sleeping Horses?

After "Let Me See the Colts" by Smog

Probably, though I can't seem to think
of any, or do anything at all, except watch

the white ones lying in the grass
like quiet unshifting clouds.

I imagine they're dreaming of running
through a fenceless field. I believe no one

ever thinks their life is enough,
which is why we dream up worlds

we will never know
are real or not: heaven, poems.

Once, my grandmother led me into a room
and lit two candles framing her late mother's picture.

I studied it for what seemed like hours wondering how,
in that barely-light, her eyes were still looking at mine.

I can't help but stare at things
tucked just beyond my reach.

I'm always looking to the sky
as if one day I'll get to see its edges,

the same sky covering the horses
like a blanket they can never shed.

Not that they'd want to. It's unfair of me to pour
my desire into animals who might wish for nothing

but a spot on the ground to rest.
And so, though I want to end the poem

with the horses rising, and their heads turning
into flames as they gallop

past the horizon, leaving
trails of ashes beneath their hooves,

I won't. I'll let them lie there,
wingless angels nuzzled in the earth.

Who am I to wake them?

Moss

First the hand grew moss. Then a forest of animals. Snakes lurking through grass. An elephant with blue skin. A dragon making small fires in a lantern. Two kids running through the tall weeds. Quick feet. Soft toes. Dry mud. Beneath them the dirt gives in to each one of their steps. One kid reaches a hand down to his feet, picks pebbles into his palm. Tosses one then another, to his brother, who opens his mouth and catches them.

My father told me that story. Though I've forgotten which character he is. Either he's moss, the pebbles, the knees of the boys, or the small fires wavering with the wind. I'm always his son, no matter what form he takes. And whether the hand is turned up at the sky, or if the palm is buried in the dirt.

SUZI F. GARCIA

What was fascinating to me about *The Wonderful Wizard of Oz*, and something I think that makes it a uniquely American fairy tale, is its commitment to disappointment. Yes, for Dorothy there is this magical place (for those unfamiliar with the series beyond the film, she eventually returns to Oz, taking her family and her favorite hen). Still, this magical place is not perfect.

There are borders in Oz. Surrounding Oz is a deadly desert, familiar to many immigrants. Tigers are wandering hungry always, because they want to eat babies but have a moral obligation not to do so. There are bad witches and selfish coups that fall apart quickly. This is not a perfect, happy place. I did not imagine that "over the rainbow" was perfect, but the important factor in these poems is that the speaker and Dorothy would be happier if they were together, no matter which side of the rainbow they end up on.

For me, the idea of Oz, with its own evils and politics and the absurdism of them all, was the kind of fantasy I could understand growing up. I never believed in the American dream. My father came over from Peru, working hard, and there was no American dream. Though this is a romantic relationship between Dorothy and the speaker, instead of a familial one, there is the same longing for a better place—and to be together ultimately. Loneliness is key to these poems in a way I felt deeply. In some ways, it's just a drive, a plane ride, a walk through deserts. But traversing those journeys is deadly. And doing so alone comes with its own pains and its own trauma.

A Dream, a Gale

I was the middle, where the southern and northern winds met, where the house still stood, an inexact center. We were torn apart at the last moment, Dorothy, and our joints unhinged. The wind was a violence that whipped my hair, and when we settled, we did not get all the right parts. My hand has never moved like the water again. A freckle on your nose I'd not seen before. This was not a condemnation; I fell, blessed. I prism in Oz, blur borders, become stateless. Dorothy, you are the last of the miracles.

Ochre runs through your veins. Breathe out:

> *gilded air.*

I started for California, made a stop at the first place there was water. I received word that there was no gold left in Hollywood: not for me, not for you.

Dorothy, it doesn't matter; we can go full burlesque if you want, a show in Vegas every night until you're ready to return to Oz. There are lights on the strip too, Dorothy, and if we have enough pisco, I'm pretty sure we can find a rainbow somewhere along the way.

I Am Itching to Ruin My Reputation

I pop my gum
in the back of churches,
started wearing big jewelry again—
anything but emeralds. Yes,
in Oz, we were dangerous, but
isn't that what made us invincible?
Dorothy, we were supposed to be
orphans together, but stuck on Earth,
I apply too much perfume, leave rooms
in wafts of musk, roots, pepper cloves,
and saffron. My hair is teased to touch
sky, and my lips peel back in a curl—
can't no one stop me now, oh no. I cut my
own tongue on the sharpness of my canines,
suck the blood loudly, smear it across
my chin. Tapping my nails on the wood of pews,
I create my own psalms. Nobody wants
to look, nobody can look away.

Confession

I admit it, there are things
I haven't escaped. I run
in an airport, even though
it doesn't matter if I miss my flight—
no one waits for me in the next city or
the next or the next. Crossing state lines,
I am pulled. I know I could find a home,
ancient and physical, in the Amazon, among tree tops
and temple sites, but I have discovered:

Folklore & myth *are* natural,
as natural as falling into
sleep under poppies, as love between you
                &   me. We have become

       historical, we are the old story now fresh.

Remember the sunsets? I hide them
in the forests. They have seen the birds flee
the loneliness; they know what is in my heart.

WANGECI GITAU

Born in Eldama Ravine, Kenya, I moved to Massachusetts when I was seven. I found out I was undocumented in high school and have spent my whole adult life unearthing who I am beneath that searing label without the privilege of returning to Eldama Ravine, not in person or through representations in arts, literature, or public discourse. As a writer, I strive to articulate the nuance in being an undocumented Kenyan, and more profoundly, an Indigenous person in the West. These poems speak to chasms, resolved or otherwise, ruptured while traversing the empire—and my attempt at creating a vessel for the diasporic angst that spills out.

"I love you" speaks to the unnamed loss of lovers speaking in colonial language. The poem begins in quotes, implying a doublespeak—one that manifests in both the public and private spheres. The speaker and their beloved share understanding of this phrase, yet meaning seems to splinter in the private world of the speaker, allowing for mistrust to seep in. The speaker's beloved is naive to how love manifests within power structures. But this youth offers hope, suggesting that this colonial world, rife with misunderstandings, is only in its primordial form and can be overcome.

"when they call me african american" uses a prose block to mimic the boxes I am placed in as an Indigenous African in the West. The list begins by unpacking the indescribable legal and existential weight that can come from being called "African American," an otherwise accurate designation. Slowly, the terms meld together, playing into juxtaposed manifestations of Blackness—the Caribbean milieu of my neighborhood bodega, the word for root vegetables in my native Gikuyu, and the images of anti-Black American violence that threaten both. There's an anticlimactic pause when I write "when I get my green card I struggle to name myself something other than a void." One might assume that getting a green card would resolve my crisis of identity. But, after being given names for decades, I lack the muscle to name myself. Triumphantly, by the bottom of the block, I regain control, finding "Agikuyu," the specific name for my tribe in our language, with the added guidance of both African and African American figures, reconciling the nebulous categories assigned by the empire, and foreshadowing an integrated Black self possible in this newly formed poetic enclosure.

"I love you"

"I love you." The words were in English. The sentiment universal enough I thought, something we had both heard of, if not experienced for ourselves. Yet I found myself using those words as a placebo for things I could not say like "how are you so desperate to belong when everything looks and smells like you" and "why me? why do you need to hear this from me?" I used the word "love" when I had nothing else. We were young in the universe. We were young to each other. We only had "love" in English.

when they call me african american, i hear the uscis agent: lips wet, sliding crisp papers across his desk and refusing me eye contact   spitting out the words "marriage fraud" "5 years" and "federal prison." when they call me negra, or morenita, i see *maembes* at their prime sitting next to aging *ngwaci* at the bodega near my house, the tv on rotating footage of the streets flooded in protest after Breonna Taylor is shot in   her own bed. when they call me Black, i see Muthoni   wa Kirima hiding in the bush from the british, hair locked, fists full of rage. when they call me free, i think of the Mau Mau refusing to cut their hair until liberation, Muthoni's 6ft long unraveling crown, ceremoniously and consensually   cut in 2022   because she wants to live again inside her 92 years   of youth and protest. when they call me strong   and woman, i think of Wangari Maathai, tied to the trees in Uhuru park, fighting for   a future where i know branches and trunks as anatomy of the ancestors, before i am robbed of my existence as anatomy of the universe. when i get my green card i struggle to name myself   something other than a void. inside my Cucu Nduta's   stories i find *Agĩkũyũ,*   of the *Anjiru* clan on my dad's side and the *Ambui* clan on my mom's. when they call me of the African diaspora, the *mugumo* tree juts its roots deeper into my veins, spreading its canopy, intelligent and wild like Angela Davis's afro, roots and   leaves yearning to reconcile something vast and universal and written brightly in my blood.

JAN-HENRY GRAY

I understand the broken line. Being undocumented trained me to see, accept, and eventually celebrate all kinds of discontinuity and disjunction. For those of us whose lives are marked by breaks in lineage—childless queers, migrants in diaspora, refugees, exiles—artmaking can help mend the "unhealable rift" of being *from* but not *of* a place. To make material of one's life into art is an attempt toward cohesion. Rick Barot writes, "I realize that the shard and not the whole / comprises a life, the image and not the narrative."

For undocumented writers, writing is both an act of forging (something new, one hopes) and a kind of forgery. Writers lie, fake, embellish, imagine, and dream in the gaps. Poems are like large rooms capacious enough to be filled with just about anything: fragments, bursts of language, and vivid observations. It's no wonder that poetry, with its profusion of broken lines, is home to so many of us.

On Your First Trip Abroad with a U.S. Passport, 44 Years Old

how you want to go back, greens with little else, suspense at customs, to prove a point, learning the pace of afternoons, gin-soaked cucumbers, black bread, handsome men, walking without taking photographs, feels like California, I'm waiting for the train, I'm on the train, window seat, from the balcony we can see the Mediterranean, soft cheese, steamed fish, how much Tagalog I heard on the streets, how cheap it was to eat, meat hung on the hook, because I'd rather not, because I was ineligible to travel like this, because I understand slowness, process, government inefficiency, smaller portions, no one drank from the tap, yes to espresso, house vermouth, wine at every hour, things fade away, more often and throughout the day, perfect pudding, the beaches, the bronzed nakedness, the newness of travel, the ethics of tourism, if it's really important you'll find out, the name of the ripe summer melon, more flight than fight, hotel room refrigerator, an empty familiarity, grilled squid, expertly prepared, how much your Spanish returned, your relationship to time and languages, how easy it all was, of course you leave the hard parts out, your deep resentment at not having seen the world, a journey reduced to an anecdote, what do you want to eat tonight, how was your trip, it's been so long

Missing Document

February 1984 / Quezon City / Philippines
Documents: copies of I-94 (missing)
Supporting Information: flight number / date of departure / seat numbers of the family members (missing)

"tell the story of somewhere else"
ISBN 978-1-56689–173

"I had a taste for ambiguity
& arrival"
ISBN 978-1-56478–184

her hand did not wave / her hand was ice / ice set to the temperature of the air / the air between the sand pressed to make the glass / the glass window she stood behind / next to the door/ the wood door / the heavy wood door that I can't say for sure was oak / but am certain was

heavy / oiled / ridged / with a gold doorknob that looked like what we were told gold looked like / gold the color not the ore / not Au or $ or what fills the vaults in the movies my mother's father watches on a Sunday / awake in the 6 am 5 am 4 am dark / his cigarette burning / a kind of dying / orange / sunrise / light /

her hand / her hand against the glass / my mother's sisters' hands / or maybe they were Maya Deren's hands / something's getting in the way / can't say / for certain / my mother's name is Rebecca // focus // tell us about her hand // what do you see // ground us // in the work // the details / go there / really take us somewhere

The Dream Act

There is A GARAGE underneath THE HOUSE.

THE HOUSE has an address.

THE GARAGE does not.

There is A DOOR cut into the garage door.

This is the entrance for THE FAMILY.

THE GARAGE is underneath THE HOUSE.

One night, THE FATHER meets another father who owns THE HOUSE.

They talk about the place downstairs, THE GARAGE underneath THE HOUSE.

THE FAMILY moves into THE GARAGE.

THE FAMILY lives there for THE YEAR.

THE GARAGE is underneath THE HOUSE.

THE FATHER brings home A TREE.

THE FAMILY calls it A CHRISTMAS TREE.

THE TREE is propped on a table in THE GARAGE.

There is no address but there is a telephone line in THE GARAGE.

THE MOTHER is on the phone with her mother.

THE MOTHER is describing THE HOUSE.

THE GARAGE is underneath THE HOUSE.

THE CHILDREN decorate THE TREE with ornaments made of paper.

ALEYDA MARISOL CERVANTES GUTIERREZ

Growing up and through my teen years I carried this feeling of being out of place. Many parts of who I was and still am were not welcome. To be an immigrant and have an accent in a majority white school. To be a young woman discovering her sexuality in a Catholic town. To want to become a writer in a low-income household.

At heart, this poem is for the people I love most in the world: my friends. Friendship became this third place full of possibility, besides my writing, another place to love and be loved no matter who you are. I have known some of my friends for over twenty-six years. We have grown up, changed, discovered new things about ourselves, encouraged each other as we enter adulthood, and laughed about our mischievousness as children. So often, as a child, I got told I was such a good kid who never did anything bad, who followed the rules and was an example to other kids. Funny enough, most of my friends said the same thing. Soon, I learned that to be good means to be loved and being myself was not an option.

For a long time, my friends and I tried to fit into this mold, whatever people wanted, the biggest people pleasers, thus always hiding parts of us. Now, as adults, we all realized how much pain we went through because of it.

When I came to writing, I was hurting. I wanted to belong somewhere, to be part of something, in writing I was able to discover this new church. Where I could create and welcome anybody. To describe with words another place where my spirit felt at peace. I think about one of my favorite songs by Queen—"I Want to Break Free"—and this is exactly how I felt writing this poem. Finally being out, finally getting to reclaim me and hoping the people I love, my friends and whoever is reading these words, can also break free.

Bad Children

Before the office jobs and endless awkward years
we used to ride bikes, cheap candy fingers holding tight

to handlebars, smelling like sweat and dirt in your mouth
racing in unpaved streets, crashing against parked cars

and the tortilla lady tells our mothers we have been
playing robbers again calling each other devil-like names

when we should be studying oh but only if she knew . . .
We are exemplary students; straight As nerds

Pink bikes with basket / two braids oversize overalls
after school community service would rather read

the entire Lord of the Rings trilogy than play a sport.
owns every Nintendo out there, math state champions

extensive vocabulary type of gang. Sunday school stars
reads the bible every church service, collects money for the poor.

Some of us dream of becoming psychologists, writers,
and even priests . . . And then children came out.

As women loving men and women, as men loving men
as me loving everyone. Despite the adults' cruelty

despite being called a problem a 'what would people say
about you' a 'but the bible says' and then your body doesn't fit

HERE TO STAY

in the house of god. The robbers are now in a therapist office
crying in each other's arms giving each other all the honey

they never got as bad children unfeeling rejection
at the hands of each other. We don't have to hold

false childhood memories We the sluts, gays, the others
We became pacifists fighting the patriarchy until our hands bleed.

We, underneath the grief of never feeling comfortable in this skin
We baptize each other in this new church nurturing ourselves

again in the name of the holy spirit.

CLAUDIA D. HERNÁNDEZ

At the age of ten, I embarked on a dangerous trip with my mother and two older sisters, guided surprisingly by decent coyotes.

Coyotes who ran alongside us through hills and parts of the desert, enduring guaguas, crowded aluminum boats on the Rio Bravo, and arranging budget motels in every Mexican city.

Leaving Mayuelas, Guatemala, we traversed Tapachula, Chiapas, to Oaxaca, then Matamoros, crossing the Rio Bravo to Brownsville, Texas, and finally reaching Southeast Los Angeles, California. The entire journey spanned twenty-one days.

Today, I remain in LA, dedicated to teaching in Southeast LA, working with immigrant children like myself. This community is where I belong, where I find purpose, and where I want to be.

My poem intertwines formalistic structures with themes of borders, rivers, and deserts in a contrapuntal exploration of hybridity versus hegemony so as to mirror border enforcement that spans physical, metaphorical, and ideological boundaries and crossings. I made use of the contrapuntal form to offer a multilayered experience challenging traditional reading practices, serving as a metaphor for navigating perspectives and the fluidity of border crossing.

My journey from a perilous border crossing to teaching in Southeast LA shapes my poem exploring form, serving as a lens to examine borders, power dynamics, and profound acts of crossing.

Border on My Side

We walked
with melted feet

chatting in
s l o w m o t i o n

our viscid
mouths

sealed
with thirst.

Our
burnt gazes

a f r a i d
to see the ghosts/

in the darkness
of the path/

in the emptiness
of dust/

until we
stumbled upon

the moist
lips of the river:

Rio Bravo
on my side,

Rio Grande
on your side.

No one
drank from

the muted
river;

our bronzed flesh
kept us warm;

as we floated
in the water

resembling
small boats

splattered
with

fresh water/
salty water.

We disembarked
on the other side—

your side,
my side.

FÉI HERNANDEZ

A state-sanctioned hunt of undocumented people calls for a people with a super (sub)conscious power. The ancestral Indigenous codes survive us, turn us into shape-shifters—in my case—into our revered kin, the deer, as my osú says. When the speculative is no longer fiction and the surveillance of ICE android canines penetrate the sacred paths of dreamwalking, the only way out is by waking through the wound-womb. The models of landscape are shaped topographically—the concentric rings of the moon, the diagonal lines of poetry—the slants of Sierra Tarahumara. Fonts, directionality of single lines, and sizes of words mock the huff and puff of being hunted. They bend into themselves for shelter as a cave, a core, or a womb. Lines bend like coiled sayáawi or trails deeper into Mother Earth and eventually, across four pages, map the eco-liminal geography of an undocumented dreamscape. The reader must engage with the callousness of hunting—the obsessive persecution—by turning the page, a physical labor, to survive an odyssey like this. The reader must rise and descend the slants of sentences with their eyes to, for a second, know the confusion and distress of a perpetual shaken focus. Hunted-bodies are not independent of the land that birthed and empowered them—these geographic portraits are the codex that I create as my descendants' continuation—and how I preserve them. A creation myth or cautionary tale—a love letter to all that has survived us in the form of a map made of words, or whatever writing poetry is.

Dreamwalk Hunt

Hoofed family, we trek the arch of watchful ceremony with bow and arrow.
Sentinel hounds are disappeared by our tree womb. They haven't launched attack.
Waterfall, frozen water braid down her kissed neck, a beautiful dream.

My subtle feet learn to harden like iron and clack against stone hands.
Upcliff, her chin, a strong jaw where the clay vase of abuela prays.
There is only bluelight in this nightwalk my sensitive dreams and I reach,

abuela, bless me
as I travel
the land that
calls me
cuz I fear to die
here too.

Horns like red
headband, my elders, I whisper with the crunch of branch,
I am afraid to be found

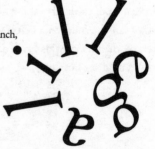

here too.

the night spills a yellow, and the green lighting betrays us.

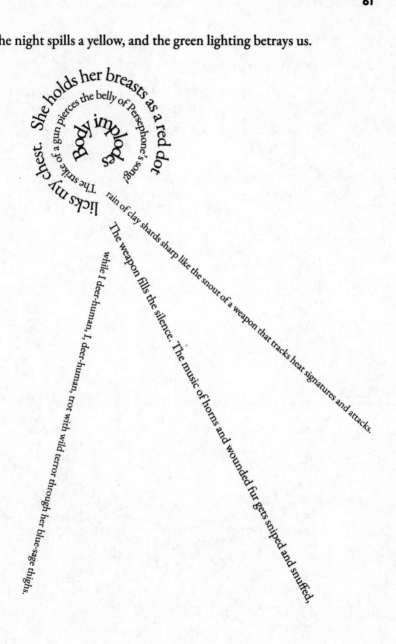

She holds her breasts as a red dot licks my chest. The strike of a gun pierces the belly of Persephone's sons. Body implodes

rain of clay shards sharp like the snout of a weapon that tracks heat signatures and attacks.

The weapon fills the silence. The music of horns and wounded fur gets sniped and snuffed,

while I deer-human, I, deer-human, trot with wild terror through her blue-sage thighs.

They chase me hungry.

the black of my rue-eyed hunted body.

Uphill, into the uterus cave of thrashing, I keep my weep in like the blood on my wounds,

Why do the narcos surround our village, abuela?

Why do the sentinel hounds find us anywhere, even in our sleep?

You told me my hoofs were wings.

My horns enough sacrilege and crown to thwart the hunter?

howls
of shots
graze
the land's
feminine

vertebrae and
I crouch and
slither
the moon is neon
and
I want to return to waking

half women, half deer,

Sierra Tarahumara turns to the window, her sigh-fog hushes the land, smogs the earth womb entry shut, lures robbers to her edges, into her canyon floors. She envelops me like love-note, presses her soul womb into me, just for me. and I refuse to die between worlds, again.

we never die.

HERMELINDA HERNANDEZ

"ID" is a confession to myself but also a letter to my family that compelled me to think about what a poem requires rather than what I want from the piece. It's not only about the struggle to renew documents and obtain some semblance of permanence, but also a way to hold on to my identity as a woman and my relationships with my family. They are essentially the backbone of my sanity and the reason I endure. This poem is a message to them, to myself, and those who can relate. "ID" is a cycle that breaks down the emotional language of traumatic experiences. It's a contrapuntal—a double identity—that allows the imagination to choose the semantic arrangement of the poem. It's an impermanently coded piece where form twists a future filled with desire. ID filters political uncertainty and syntactically cyclones all the labels swirling within me. The cold grammar of immigrant linguistics, the backward-forward-ness of words, and the abbreviations—which stand in contrast to the aesthetics of poetic form—mirrors the undocumented imagination as I see it. This is an ID as in: "I don't want to live without my family." ID as in: a nonreturn from one landscape to another enacted inside a rhetoric of power where anti-immigration language reduces undocumented people to in/animate objects.

As my own family has witnessed, the law imposes a repetition of process, a repetition of renewal, after which we are still nonetheless handcuffed, chased, and reduced to nightmares.

ID

IDon't wanto dednarbe: unconstitutional deadly
animal tneloivicious criminal IDon't wanto be
dehumanized orenew Daca every 2 yrs paying
   495 justo get a work permit & thenot be
   guaranteed safety or listen ehto other end of
   thenohp say we only hire citizens & then
   hang up IDon't wanto go to places &
   have peoplerats when I walk or sit down or
   be leftuo from things only citizens are
   privileged IDon't wanto hear rehtomy
   sayou have to marry a white man to be
   accepted or earn myaw through pity or have
   nightmares of being chasedby largìm or
   esohwitness next how many degachildren
   how many familieseparated or er'ewhen
   huntedown IDon't want us to berased heck,
IDon't want us to be hunted or asummarized
stnargimmillegal undocumented saliens
if erewe things & not people

IDon'tanw otravel with orestriction advancedparole
or pay a crazy amount I can't afford & when I apply
IDon't wanto know there's a big chance I mighton
be approved or if IDo   IDon't wanto know
it's because of abuela sawho deportedback
tOaxaca nowho hasetebaid whose
recent photo reminds me of a skeleton & I
knowriting this won't bring me any closer
whato I want & what I want is completely
different from reality causelpoep like us
have nother choice buto gon & if fone usi
gone s'erehthen no point in continuing
this absurd charade I wanto be

   f   r   e   e   s   t

buthesearethingsican'tdismantle

MARCELO HERNANDEZ CASTILLO

Although both the poems "If Found, Then Measured" and "Field Guide Ending in a Deportation" were written around the same time, and in a similar vein, "Field Guide" was the last poem I wrote in the wreckage of my addiction to alcohol and other substances while "If Found" was the first sober poem I wrote in the throes of early withdrawal. Like many other people who lack access to health care, I, too, found other ways to cope and heal; and if not to heal, at least to temper the feelings of helplessness that hardened into rage in my stomach. In my addiction, I didn't see how self-medicating was a problem, I saw it as a limited solution among limited choices. Poetry, however, never felt like a choice, but rather an imperative; that is, until drinking, too, stopped feeling like a choice, which made the poetry harder and harder to come by. Although there was poetry in both my addiction and sobriety, I am making the choice to revoke the myth that great art must come from great suffering. I don't want to hurt anymore, but I will also never forget the hurting.

Field Guide Ending in a Deportation

I confess to you my inadequacies. I want to tell you things I do not know about myself. I've made promises to people whom I will never see again. Once, I cried in an airport bathroom stall in El Paso, TX, when immigration denied my father's application. It felt like a mathematical equation—everything on one side needed to equal everything on the other. It almost made sense to be that sad. I am not compelled to complicate this metaphor. I'm selling this for two dollars. Years ago, on my birthday, I came out to my friends. I thought about the possibility of painting their portraits. What a stupid idea. I've started to cover up certain words with Barbie stickers in my journal. It occurs to me, sitting in my car, at a Dollar General parking lot, in search of cheap balloons for a party which I do not care about, that I am allowed my own joy. I pick the brightest balloons, pay, drive home and dress for the party. I mouth the words *happy birthday to you* in a dark room lit by everyone's phone cameras. Afterward, I enter all of my emails from five years into a cloud engine and the most used word is *ok*. I confess that I have had a good life. I spend many nights obsessing over the placement of my furniture. I give you my boredom. I give you my obligation. I give you the night I danced and danced and danced at a child's birthday party, drunk and by myself. I've been someone else's shame. It's true, at its core, amá was deported because she was hit by a car. For years to come, this will be the ending of a sad joke she likes to tell. I laugh each time she tells the joke to strangers. Something about how there is more metal than bone in her arm. Something about a magnet. She says *I thought I had died and death meant repeating a name forever.* She says *el jardín encierra la boca de mis pasos.* But this is a bad translation. It's more like *I felt like a star, I felt like somebody famous.*

If Found, Then Measured

1.
Now that I can, I am afraid to become a citizen.
I am arriving, and departing,
and later I will punish myself for looking over
at the person sitting next to me on the plane,
and reading their email.
For now there is no punishment.
I realize everyone is just as boring as me.
Everyone in TSA has enormous hands.
I still refuse to travel with my green card.

2.
It is my mother's birthday and
I bought her merchandise from a school
I didn't attend but only visited.
She, too, understands
the value of cultural capital.
Today I am *wounded*.
I like to say *wounded* instead of *sad*.
Sadness is reserved for days
when I can actually make money.

My mother raised me
to make sure nothing I ever did
I did for free.

3.
When I land, Northern California is burning.
We keep a suitcase near the door just in case.
A man calls my child three
different names before giving up

and asks if he has begun coughing yet.
I do not answer.
Beneath all the ash,
no one seems bothered
if you cry in public.

Eight months sober,
sitting around a circle
of other grateful alcoholics,
some of whom will leave the room
with a clearer portrait of their ruin,
which, depending on who you ask,
can either mean they will
or will never return,
I say what I need to say and
a man tells me I am selfish. I am.

Sometimes I want every goddamn piece of the pie.

4.
A woman pulls aside her mask to smoke and says
she's going to look up at what temperature
teeth begin to melt, the implication being
that if teeth can melt in a wildfire,
they won't be able to identify her parents
who are still missing up the hill in Paradise.
When I pray, I don't know who I am talking to yet.
I take the eucharist in my mouth for the first time
since changing religions and it is not as holy as I imagined.

4.
How easy. How effortless. This breath.
I'm here. I'm here. I'm right here. I want to say.
I wish things were simple,

HERE TO STAY

like taking just one drink and not another,
like not burning in a fire,
like letting things be good without being holy.
I wouldn't have to pretend to try
to resume the bounty of this blossom.

Cenzontle

Because the bird flew before
    there was a word
    for flight

        years from now
        there will be a name
      for what you and I are doing.

I licked the mango of the sun—

between its bone and its name
between its color and its weight,

    the night was heavier
    than the light it hushed.

Pockets of unsteady light.

    The bone—
    the seed
  inside the bone—

      the echo
    and its echo
    and its shape.

Can you wash me without my body
coming apart in your hands?

    Call it *wound*—
    call it *beginning*—

HERE TO STAY

The bird's beak twisted
    into a small circle of awe.

    You called it cutting apart,
        I called it song.

SAÚL HERNÁNDEZ

For me using images, objects, or geographical location to juxtapose against each other is what helps create the tension throughout my poems. In graduate school, I was able to attend an intimate talk with Jericho Brown. In that roundtable he expressed how he juxtaposes violence and tenderness throughout most of his work to create the poems' desired tension. This element of juxtaposition has been embedded into most of my writing. Through these two poems I juxtapose the relationship of beauty to dangerous landscape and the beauty of films to reality. My relationship to beauty, as a poet, is I tend to look at even the smallest details to magnify them in my work such as a frog canister or the landscape in general. Having lived in the sister cities of Ciudad Juárez, Chihuahua, Mexico, and El Paso, Texas, USA, I found beauty in the desert cactus and endless dryness where most people only see danger.

Surrealism for me is necessary in my work because I'm always wondering *what if.* Since I was a child whenever I found myself in an unpleasant situation or event, I not only began imagining a story, but I would summon it, I'd daydream about the illogical things happening, such as a tornado happening in the middle of my school day, launching me into an alternative reality where nothing makes sense. As an adult I know this is a trauma response. This has helped push my work as a poet in creating scenes where my poems offer not only dreamlike situations but also question truth and seek answers. However, now I know sometimes to survive we must transform ourselves into objects or creatures defying logic—to write toward the realms of possibilities.

When Tío Juan Bloomed

Tío Juan swears he once swallowed the sky out of thirst.
  He had been walking for three days, el coyote left him behind
      with water in a 16 oz frog canister.

He finished it before the end of the first day.
  The second day he woke up in a field of bright roses.
      Tío Juan plucked till his fingertips dripped with blood.

He gathered all the petals, bathed with them & with the wetness of his blood.
  The next day, he woke up to la migra pouring water on him & fanning him.
     He was sitting in their truck.

He kept repeating *¿Ya estoy en el otro lado?*
  As they drove, he thought he saw himself as a rose,
    the sky pouring into him.

The Last Video Store

The first man to lie to me was Apá

Aquí siempre encontrarás magia.

At a video store I became obsessed with the stories each videotape held
inside. For seven years I collected movies to escape this world.

When we didn't have money to eat, we exchanged videotapes for money
at the nearby pawn shop. I didn't know movies could nourish our bellies too.

$3 per videotape they would give us. We'd make sure to take five movies so
in return we get $15 enough for two Hot-N-Ready pizzas & a two-liter Pepsi.
Apá would look at me after the man would give him the money, *No te preocupes
siempre habrán más películas.*

The person at the pawn shop would examine every tape as if it was going
into an operation, opening the film cartridge to look for damages, they would
look at the video's box & make sure the plastic or cardboard wasn't bent or worn
out.

Apá collects movies now. At every thrift store he buys one, adding to his
collection. What used to be my old room houses his videotapes. Apá has be-
come the last video store & I'm still waiting for magic to save us.

PATRYCJA HUMIENIK

When I'm writing, I try to feel my feet. Though I don't resist abstraction entirely, I find ideas to be most alive when embodied and relational. I am moved by the sensuous material of our daily lives. William Carlos Williams wrote, "No ideas but in things." For me, it's: No ideas but in each other. No ideas but in our bodies.

I am the daughter of formerly undocumented Polish immigrants, from a country that's been taken off the map, whose borders have been drawn and re-drawn over centuries. Borders lie—we belong not to nations but to each other and ourselves. Poetry is the space where I can turn every word, over and over, as it catches light and shadow. What do we mean when we say: self, nation, belonging? Who is we? In "You Are Who I Love," Aracelis Girmay offers a poetics of seeing and being with each other, of widening the boundaries of we, of our love, that I aspire to.

Figuration

My lover with the cello between his knees, bow hovering

There's a place we go when we talk about empire

It is not abstraction

When I try to help my father prepare for the citizenship test he says, *That's not one of the questions*

Gas nearing $7 a gallon

My mother doesn't miss a day of work

Leftovers wedged in the widened space between my gums and the fake tooth

My father calls me his American dream

A good daughter is a secret keeper

I suppose I am to live like a kind of evidence

Salt of the Earth

In a blurry photo from my first trip to Poland at 19, me and my godmother, one of my mother's ten siblings, are laughing together, a thousand feet into the earth, in a 13th-century chapel made entirely of salt. Sculptures carved of rock salt, rock salt chandeliers, a rock salt Last Supper.

In childhood, she was one of many names.
A voice on the phone. A formal exchange.

Table salt was made there from the upwelling brine. Upwelling the closest thing resembling a wall in water.

*

I feared the door. Someone coming to take
my parents away.

Illegals—Taking
American jobs—

In classroom debates about immigration,
I kept quiet.

*

Watching my godmother watch her grandchildren running the edges of the creek I wanted to call a river. Slicing bugs from mushrooms picked before dawn. Dropping the slivers quick into buckets. Asking when will I have children, and haven't I had enough school already, and how is it that we have so much debt in America?

*

Shielded by whiteness,
assumed to be documented.

Threaten the economy—One out of every 12 newborns—

*

In another aunt's kitchen, over rosehip tea, she said I wasn't as spoiled as they'd expected, for an amerykanka. I was proud, and devastated to be called American.

*

Providing an advantage to family members seeking to secure citizenship—

Silence both protected and betrayed.

*

At 22, running up a blur of pines, beyond my uncle's turkeys and geese, to where my mama grew up picking blueberries, I planted a little tree. Where I'm invited to return.

*

The difference between a river and a creek is that
from a creek, no new branches are formed.

Anchor baby, n. Offensive

We

who am i   to speak

for anyone   but my

many selves

here: this page: fingers running over: you: yes, you, dear

reader: have we—   do i—   know you?

we? as in all bodies? ever

touched: in passing: past: i was born
an ocean away from   where i was conceived   circling a prayer:
longing   bending over, under   how water goes: grief
pooling in my clavicles:

&   all   who   came before:
is we a home?

who is not
here: left   out:

in Spanish: nosotros: otro:
as in other

when i learn a language not spoken in my family
am i trying to expand the we?

we is my   in Polish   the y softer
not possession: it's not mine

to belong to: be longed for   is we   a longing

ALEJANDRO JIMENEZ

In one of the last scenes of Billy Luther's *Frybread Face and Me*, the main character, Benny, is preparing to return to the city after spending a summer on the Navajo Reservation with his grandmother, uncle, and cousin. Benny, now the adult narrator, states, "As a kid you think everything will be in its place when you return." I left my country when I was eight years old. I didn't say goodbye to my friends. We were rushing to catch the truck that would drive us out of our hometown. I returned as an adult. After spending time with my family, I walked toward the almond tree, just a few houses from my childhood home. The tree had been cut down. My friends had emigrated. Some within my country, others out of it. In my everlasting wondering of *what I left behind or what was denied to me*, coming to this country, I think about the almond tree and the endless marble games I played and witnessed. It was the first place where I saw young men and boys express care in such a gentle and tender way without the fear of being judged. I returned, filled with joy and also wounded. I longed for everything, and everyone, to be where I had left them. Memory, and poetry, reminds me that I can return, not just to a physical place, but also into the humanity that toxic masculinity seeks to keep from me.

Marbles

We played marbles underneath the branches of the almond tree while the birds sang. If your marble was hit out of the square of play or if it was hit more than a spread-palm's length away from its original spot, you lost that marble. You could play the game with as many marbles as was agreed upon beforehand. We would also bet an X number of marbles per game. We would play like this under the almond tree until the top of our thumb would be tender from using it as a trigger to shoot our marble into other marbles. When one of us wanted to quit before all of our marbles were pushed out or hit far away, we would hold out our thumb for the other players to examine. If it was decided that it was not tender enough—by how it looked or by how it felt or by the lack of blood—one would still have to play. This is the masculinity I used to know: boys caressing each other's hands making sure that we were not too hurt to stop listening to the birds sing.

JANINE JOSEPH

I was a senior in high school when I learned that I was without papers, and it was within those months that I watched the 2001 iteration of the DREAM Act fail. In the waiting for Godot–kind of waiting that passed, I navigated college and government forms and studied the news and election cycle—all formulaic and without variation to their patterns.

When I became a naturalized citizen, twenty years after my arrival by plane to this country, I had done so without time for contemplation or conflict. I had to act. I put on my oxygen mask first so I could then do the same for my family. For my friends and for those, I believed, I had still to meet. I crossed the threshold from one status to another in the middle of a workday, returning to the classroom, where I was a teacher, without fanfare.

After a catastrophic car crash in 2008, I crossed another threshold in the indeterminate years of my post-concussive recovery. While losing my memory, I navigated insurance and immigration forms. Before I knew it, I had come to and was documented.

What does it mean to have cleared the path begun by my parents? How does it feel to have survived the wreck? To have directed myself, somehow, here? Across the threshold too are mysteries. I write into what I can't and can't yet name. I bend to the demands of its syntax, adjust myself to its vantage point. It is a familiar, formal challenge to tell a perforated story, to evoke the intangible, to be so uncertain.

In the Ecotone

2019

Only when and only when I
                     develop heart palpitations—wake
as if undead from sleep—
              do I remember being motioned
by wand from the mass
           arms akimbo through security

As we were split into different
                 lines I said to my father en route
to take his Oath of Allegiance
              See you on the other side
as he was quickened
          out then out of sight

I observed the room as not
             a room but an exhibition hall
an arena of partitions
          as it with thousands that morning
in September across the news
         tumefied with family and friends

Behind me someone *Years ago*
          said *You could stroll right*
through without procession *Without*
           this wait my god—
You just showed up—so
        so great we got here when we did

My metals unfastened and
                 conveyed I crossed Janine
beneath the detector's flat arch
                 and appeared again Janine
without alarm or search
                 in the same fluorescence

Wholly I walked but imagined
                 I fizzed or interfered made a sound
like static between stations
                 or my body like a hologram
on the sensor threshold zigzagged
                 coming in and out then clear

What possessions I gathered
                 from the belt were pulsed though
with waves and until I was signaled
                 elsewhere I found myself lost
looking with familiarity
                 at the slate gray flooring

It was of a shade similar
                 to the teeming lot on which I stood
when I eight years before became
                 a new American alone
who renounced and renounced
                 but did not in me feel the difference

I had for a time been from
                 form to form to form
unaccompanied in my ascent
                 so had supposed for a spell
I should for the duration also
                 as they say *go at it alone*

HERE TO STAY

What did I remember of driving
                              homeward back to work
after my naturalization but myself
                              in my car dashing
singly like lines on the road
                              reflecting in perpetuity

I lingered in the echo until
                              like a shield I was moved
next into the atrium where
                              from a distance scored
yellow with caution tape
                              my father raised and flagged his arm

And until the court with a flick
                              fell dim we could see him
make with his fingers the sign
                              of peace meaning *two* as in
And then there were two or
                              as in *And now two more*

Epithalamium Ending in Divorce

You were bothered, I could tell, through the pomp,
the vows, their kiss's soft applause. At the late reception
of fairy lights in mason jars, you were a strobe of looks
and looked at while you tongued the open bar dry.
I held you up in the melody because you were mine
the way the country in you was mine. Two crooks
hung around my shoulders in the sway. An affection,
I could see, the way you let me see the wells grow damp.

Decade of the Brain

> "The boundaries of a CDP have no legal status and may not always correspond
> with the local understanding of the area or community with the same name."
> —*Wikipedia*, "Census-designated place"

Alone from my porch, through the tick-thick grass

      and into the street suffused with mammatus light,
I walk. No birds call, but the gale pulls chimes

from the wood. Days and nights with the movers pass

    and I make a career of anticipating
        on the buckled blacktop a tornado to descend

like a spine and distort the field. It is mine now,

a yard among yards where neighbors hedge their cars
    crosswise and the steel blooms at solar noon. Mine,

      the salaried life my parents scrounged for, one can

    at a time in the shopping cart we raucoused
for miles down graveled roads like these.

I can see it through the glare: Pedley, California,

      1991. My first fall in the decade of *understanding
and discovering our selves* as Americans. The little we knew

we balanced on a wobbly, folding wicker chair,

        changing the channels by hand with a knob
                until the electricity shut off and the pool scourged

        with mosquitoes. Clear still, the ringing of pennies rained

from their pockets into the three-foot-tall glass jar
        centered in the home like a hearth. I can see it

        though my searches load our disappearance

        from the map. In history, we exist only in the count,
our bodies a record of a place absorbed

        by ink. But I was witness. I watched their teeth,

        their hair fall out in clenches I temper
now, here, on this plain far and away

from each of them, where decades have done nothing

        but landscape the landscape. Still, still—
        they are here as I am, landlocked

as I remember it.

JOËL SIMEU JUEGOUO

I monopolized the head of the kitchen table growing up, where I did all my work. So, I was the first to greet my mother, who surprised us with treats—dark chocolates, kiwis, the occasional McChicken.

Always with an eye for a good deal, she once came home midweek with boxes of chickens from a farm. I was incredulous when she asked me to help her prepare them. How would I convey the feathered bloodbath scene unfolding in our kitchen to my friends at school?

But the chickens sustained us that winter. And when I consider the challenge of raising my brothers and me, I feel a reverence toward my mother. Reverence for the way she nurtured us in this foreign country. Reverence for the miracle of her meals, which kept us warm, close, and loved.

This poem is an ode to the lineage of "sweaty brows" and "greased elbows" inherent to the women of my family. I would not be who I am without their fortitude and their love.

Sous-chef

we unplucked them
in a crowded kitchen—
slit their sternums open and watched,
mouths agape and noses plugged
as blood painted the carpeted floor
with sweaty brows and greased elbows,
I marveled at how the boiling water
blanched them all so quickly
their raw exterior,
softening with each bubbling wave.
That bitter Pennsylvanian winter,
my mother brought home 10 chickens
with their feathers still intact
I witnessed her
turn meager into magic

mothering into
a queer sort of sorcery

TOBI KASSIM

In *The Undercommons*, Fred Moten and Stefano Harney develop the idea of fugitivity as a constant state of motion that "cuts the regulative, governant force of (the) understanding."[5] My English professor, David Kaufmann, further described fugitivity as the feeling that something moved out of the corner of your eye before you could see it. I often associate this image with the feeling-space of Deferred Action for Childhood Arrivals (DACA), an immigration status of temporary exemption that transgresses a rigid border or binary between "legal" and "illegal" status.

DACA requires the state's surveillance of the movements and speech of its recipients, but it creates new potential for escape at the edges of surveillance's notice. My indeterminate status reaffirms my faith that something that defies categorization lives in our survival. The shame and fear of undocumented status stifled my family's ability to communicate. We endured a long fracture in the idea of family as my younger brother and sister were not allowed to immigrate to America.

Poetry offers me a space of freedom where more truthful understandings of my kinship with others and with our world can emerge. Between being "documented" or "undocumented" lives a potential way of being that does not rely on violent inventions like "borders" for belonging. I resist the law's regulations of movement to celebrate moments that reconcile my geographically severed family, and to recognize the struggles that intertwine my life with those who seem different from me. Poetry travels beyond the borders that documentation reifies in our thinking. I try to catch what is moving outside these boundaries, and ask how we can get there.

Family Stone

When they asked my daddy for i.d. I showed them mine.
When we needed blades & generators to light the granite
factory's operations. I vouched my name for those rentals,
my murky illegitimacy. When the table saw sliced
through stone, water flooded the cuts and all
the words I've written ran through the sluices, heavy
gray slurry, with twinkles every now and then. A slate
lake catching the night sky. I felt elastic those evenings; we'd cut
templates of strangers' kitchens until after mommy called
about dinner. I learned to measure the lines endurance draws
out of these long hours, crawling to set the seams in place,
creases in the stone patience of our prayers. Pant legs starched bone
white with dust we'd wear off the factory floor. That year
with you was just a taste of earth's slow erosion in my lung;
silica, mica, small knives iridescent in the fading light.
I hear a quartzite cuts in your chest when you cough dust
out of sleep. I think your wings must be alabaster by now
blooming your bronchial flowers. Occasionally a mistake
rings my phone. A credit company asks for you: You mean my
dad? I inflect. Deflect whatever debt they call to collect. I lie.
All of it is surely mine.

A Blind Spot, Awash

And if I give up on consequences
is that despair
or passion? I can't protect
myself from either. The lantern swinging
bearing down, pressing the dark
to a sliver
of shade at the edges of my field
of vision. My body alight in
the seat of this question and indecisive—
if to be moved through,
             de-throated,
the groove in the thoroughfare.

I felt reduced waking up

crumpled by the water, an amniotic curve
along the shore. My only shape
was having been carried,
left at rest. And everything
I thought I could lose—
when I followed the rushes back, resurfaced.

Wings tucked just so or grasses threaded
gently from ear to ear, rewiring their small
skulls. I understood the first mercy
      of diving is blindness, those parachutes blooming
             the drag that yanked me back
to my body, almost touching my lungs.

The Alien/nation/body in search of wings

I bellied the high wire a faint buzzing
strung between my legs. Like a signal. I sidled
along the power line on my belly, relayed
and swooping low at points, swinging
I slid across the sky gripping tightly the power
line, my home among the smog I thought, song
my home among birds. The crows slung my new
name low over the porches, cooing
don't let me fall, the voice settling in the invisible
net strung between the power lines.
I peered down from the wire, so much
falling held slightly off the ground—
the hum of entanglement our steps just
hovered over. the buzz of containment
barely escaped. I was strung between the poles
stretching to be everywhere. *Let me belong
to everybody now*, thought teetered, I can make
this string vibrate, I can see the warp of that
sound no one really hears anymore.

JANE KUO

I carry with me, always, a compendium of voices. Poetry is my Sisyphean attempt at excavating and recontextualizing these voices. In this way, my poems are a reenactment, a soundtrack on repeat, a haunting.

In "Chinese Bodies, American Cars," I examine how something as ubiquitous and seemingly innocuous as a car—and yes, something so American—can be a portal to understanding trauma. I write in the second person because that is when I'm least afraid. I write in the second person because I do not need permission to speak to myself.

I am both the speaker and the audience, and everyone else is just eavesdropping. And when someone is an eavesdropper, they don't really have a right to anything, do they? It's a privilege to receive whatever little bits they can glean, and that's how I want the listener to feel, like a trespasser made privy to something intimate.

Intimate, but not pleasant: I want my words to sound like wrong notes at a piano concerto, I want the listener to protest, *no no no that's not my experience*, I want them to squirm.

My poems present the reader with a choice: come here and sit with me or choose not to be implicated, to remain on the outside, eavesdropping.

Chinese Bodies, American Cars

It's 1982, your mother tells you about Vincent Chin, a man beaten to death in Detroit.

Two men took a baseball bat to his head, two men upset about American auto workers getting laid off. They blamed the Japanese auto industry. They thought Vincent Chin was Japanese.

Your mother tells you: *Vincent Chin is Chinese, the Japanese and the Chinese are not the same, but in this country, they think we are.* The killers were fined $3000 and ordered to serve three years' probation. The other details of the story that your mother told you, that you never forgot: Vincent Chin was an only child, he died four days before his wedding day.

Three years later, when it's time to buy a second car, your father insists on *buying American.*

His first car was a Datsun 210. That car served the family well but Dad wanted an American car, because he loves America and he thinks that buying a Buick is a way to show his love. But the Buick was a lemon. It sucked up more money in repairs after just a few years than all the money he ever put into the Datsun.

It's 1988, your sister crashes the blue Buick when she loses control of the power brakes.

You're sitting in the passenger seat. Linda keeps applying the brakes but the car does not stop and she hits a Volvo during stop-and-go traffic. This breaks your dad's heart. He writes a letter to General Motors telling them *something is wrong with the car.* It's full of grammatical errors. He wants you to proofread the letter. You're a teenager at the time, you roll your eyes, tell him, *why bother?* He mails off the letter anyway.

HERE TO STAY

It wasn't until 2014 when you read about General Motors recalling over 15 million vehicles that you thought about Dad's letter. There was something wrong with that blue Buick and General Motors never responded to your father.

Your father died in 2002.

ESTHER LIN

As a young reader, I was stymied by Yeats and "No Second Troy." Who was Maud Gonne? What were the little streets, hurled upon the great? It was a complicated political situation. I wanted Yeats to add to the poem's formal requirements the whole burden of explaining history. Later on, I understood I, too, was in a unique political situation, of which I was one small character. Smaller than, but not unlike Maud, Helen. To satisfy a reader like my younger self, each of my poems would have to explain United States immigration policy and why its victims remain shadowy.

Like other American artists, I was transformed by a sojourn in Paris. Here I was indisputably American. My mannerisms, my accent—an undocumented immigrant who worked so hard to appear brilliantly assimilated now discovered she had no guise but an American one! This was a very funny inside joke that I tried to explain to mystified Europeans. In Paris, I was not undocumented. In Paris, I was my most fundamental self: an artist.

I was also liberated rhetorically. The burden of having to explain history fell away. The poem "French Sentence" is, to me, French because while writing it I discovered I no longer needed to utter only one kind of sentence—the kind born of the fear and shame of my immigration status. I discovered I could speak to my undocumented kinsmen without any attention to passersby.

Season of Cherries

First the pink ones, with yellow lights.
Then the silky dark ones.
Sweeter, nearly cloying as you and I
eat and eat until the bag folds over.
My first knowledge was tell no one.
This is love among the undocumented.
Tell no one. When I met you, even you,
I wondered, would you do it?
In the courtyard the dust rises.
Soon there will be peaches, plums.
I am ready for them all.
My mother says, *Well, what did you
expect*. Deportation is deportation.
Heartbreak is heartbreak. They
shouldn't be the same to us.
No rain, it turns out. You and I sleep
awhile, make love before the moon sets.
The shadows of each eyelash dive
like swifts down your cheek.
Attention to detail is a survivor's trait.
Will you marry me is one question.
Will you report me is the other.

Citizen

As a child I relied on my mother and my father.
I could not have relied on anyone else.

As a young woman I relied on my husband.
Who provided what my parents could not.

With a man, or was it a green card, I changed.
Now I could move. Speak. Be seen. Be heard.

My apparition was cunning.

*Watch her attend university. Watch her fall in love
with a man not her husband.*

*How lifelike! How womanly!
Her maker must be praised.*

Wedding; interview; civics exam.
All triumphs. My name was known.

My husband refused an equal divide

in our divorce. If I knew right
from wrong I would ask for less.

*Her parents are dead. She cared for them
but she was angry. They died alone.*

Alone I traveled. Alone I worked.
The gray skies of Rouen were not the gray skies

of London. The Seine was not like the East. Soon
I would learn more. When to use metaphor

and when to speak plainly. There was no one
to represent me. I had only myself.

French Sentence

for Marcelo and Janine

My teacher tells me, madame
we cannot write that you wept in public
more than once. This is

not a French sentence.
Instead let us write that you were moved
to action.

For revolutionaries smashed
the stone face of the Virgin
with the stone face of Saint Denis—

The Virgin a lover, finally!

On streets, I place my hand
inside pocks
shot into limestone walls. In bookshops,

lithographs burn palaces, carriages,
and children. The check-in girl refuses
my identification card.

Okay. This year I've enough
nods and stamps that this
does not hurt me. For I have left America.
I have left America!

ANNI LIU

Like so many undocumented or otherwise-precarious young people, I was raised to avoid danger at all costs. I was schooled in how to be safe, and simultaneously, how to be afraid. This often meant being quiet, lying low, and staying vigilant. None of this kept me from coming into danger, and in fact, as I learned, it's your loved ones who often hurt you most. But for so long that information didn't make sense in my body. I couldn't comprehend how this hurt had been possible, and there was often no acknowledgment from others that harm had taken place at all. My poems are a place where I try to make sense of that. They ask for witness, where witness means a sustained attention to something that may feel unbearable. This includes injury at the hands of the state, my family, my peers, myself. This includes the victimization of those who have hurt me. This includes my own cruelty, cruelty disguised as love. This also includes beauty, forgiveness, and agency. What would it mean to release the idea of constant protection? To stop playing it safe and instead to claim the risks we mean to take?

The Story

I was born in Xī'ān, a three-thousand-year-old city encircled by walls.

Before I arrived, my mother visited me in dreams: A girl. My father's hair. My mother's mouth.

She waited, devouring shrimp and green apples.

Seven years later, she left.

My father bought a red motorcycle. It gleamed, gold specks in red enamel.

My grandparents moved into the campus apartment where my mother's books were still stacked, and my father stayed on the other side of town.

Sun fell through knotted curtains. The moon visited us in turn.

In summer, the road out of campus kicked dirt in our faces. Sweat mixed with dirt made a new and tougher skin.

In winter, motorcycle rides with white cotton face masks and stiff wool coats. The air's silt like snow.

I heard her voice on the telephone: "Where do you miss me?" But I could not locate *missing* in my body.

(Why document this, as if forgetting were the worst thing.)

The ocean came to my city once, city once mine.

City so dry and ill-equipped that any hard rain will make it flood.

It was no ocean. Just the sky.

If your city floods with streets like asphalt riverbeds, carry your child to piano lesson on your back. Wear shower slippers, the only waterproof shoes you own. Be prepared for nails. A long nail. The arch of the foot.

                          Another time: me fevered for days, my mother gone,

my father took me to work. He spread couch cushions on the floor of the office for me to lie on, asked me what I needed.

"Tell me a story," I said.

He never told stories, but that day, he told me this:

It has a happy ending. The bunnies find their way home to their mother.

But her eyes, exhausted of tears, have fallen to the ground. Trees have sprung up where they landed, trees with eyes in their bark.

My mother never came back. Instead, I went to her, to Ohio and lead skies.

After the story was over—the rabbits sheltered under the eye trees—my father covered me with a thin blanket.

I had fallen asleep.

He could go back to work.

Night Swim at Shadow Lake

I can barely swim but I don't tell them that.
At the beach, the brothers joke about leeches
longer than my hand. They strip

and hoot with pleasure as they leap off
the slick rock. I keep my underwear on,
feel my way in, the rocks becoming dirt

then a soft sucking silt. Without my glasses,
the lake surface gleams, oiled with stars.
Someone told me once to imagine the water

holding me up to the air, buoyant,
but all I do is sink. The lake's long fingers
plug my ears, grip me like a hand closing.

Panicked, I plash back to the shallow muck
and wait. In the car back to the farm,
I sit with towel stuffed between my legs.

No one tells any jokes. In the tensed
silence, I realize they'd meant for me
to take off all my clothes. I roll down

my window, let in the night and its shrill
insect trills, its sharp slaps of wind. My entire life,
I have been afraid of the wrong things.

Six years old, my classmates and I

believe we invented this game of jumping
    from great heights, of punishing our bodies
for their softness. As if, by sustaining enough pain,
    we could be tumbled tough and world-proofed
against hurt. I am young enough to still believe
    that old saying about eating bitterness.

But there is one girl who refuses to play.
    Standing on the edge of the cement stage,
she wears a dress the color of whitefish
    open on a butcher board. The skin on
her face seems brand new, never ruined
    by sun, by exertion, by the gritty yellow dirt.

She would have to learn how to fall.
    The crowd of our classmates gathers beneath us.
Their hard little faces like mine, smeared with snot
    and dirt, our red scarves a knot at our throats—
and my hands find her shoulders, pillowy and warm.
    All it takes is one quick shove:

she is free of the stage and sailing,
    pale arms akimbo, soft whimper
of surprise, to land face first against the ground.
    When the teacher reaches her,
asking *who did this to you*, her mouth is choked
    full of blood and no one dares say

that it is my name she repeats like a drowned song,
    but I know: it was me, it was me, it was me.

LINETT LUNA TOVAR

After a fourth cross-country move and an imminent family-home eviction, i found myself sifting through a plethora of my belongings, spanning over twenty years. Though i approached the task with my penchant for minimalism, i found that as an undocumented person, i couldn't afford to discard hardly any of the hundreds of papers that surrounded me. "Because what if . . ."

In the process, i came across past versions of me: kid linett who was taught to base her self-worth on academic achievements; teen linett who held on to every award she received because she thought it could somehow help her pay for college as an undocumented student (or maybe even get her legal residency some day?!). i can laugh or cry about those delusions, depending on the day.

This poem is a meditation on how a piece of paper can bring us hope or crush us; how it can grant us freedom or imprison us. It is also a tribute to undoc friends, family, and strangers who have had different "paper experiences" from mine, even as we share a legal status. i am understanding that it takes a lot of discernment, honesty, and self-reflection to identify what is truly important to us, versus that which we cling to because we were made to believe it is important. May we each discover what our Truth is.

why undoc families keep so many papers

in case they ask for them.

for comedic irony.

in case you end up detained and they want to know
exactly what you were doing on july 7th, 2002.

for when they ask for proof
that you weren't another leech:
that you had bills, and you paid your dues.

because what if . . .

to show continuous presence
from now back to 1992
because the law they make someday might read
"only prior to 1993."

because you never know,
can't be too sure,
so you keep originals, 2 copies, and the certificate of mailing, too.

to own something.

because we store and wait,
store and wait,
store and wait in case
at last the government
makes one of their trading card games:
4 unbreached leases for a driver's license,

6 w-2s for a family visit,
10 tax filings for an i-94 arrival form,
500 pay slips for one social security number.
how could we not die
to collect them all?

to hold on.

because we hope
someday a ton
of our wood pulp can weigh an ounce of theirs.

for when the day finally comes.

because we'll study this archival bible for judgment day:
that sacrosanct interview hour that defines your fate.
may we be delivered from the evils
of no pension or health care in old age.

for when you lose yourself
and need to hold your childhood
portrait on your right hand, birth certificate on the left,
reciting "i am a person,
i am a person. i cannot forget."

for when you do 8 regular plus 3 overtime
hours of no one looking you in the eye or knowing your name,
then you can read a handwritten note
from your ailing mom,
and confirm you're not a ghost.

for when you run out of beer
you can gulp down an old father's day

HERE TO STAY

card from a child and wife you haven't seen
in three years or thirteen,
and help you fall asleep.

for when the evening news bring a cold front
that freezes over your hope,
then you can wrap up in a blanket
of your children's awards and feel warmth.

because the souvenirs, the ticket stubs,
the photographs,
and the fading boarding pass
remind us of the first time we flew
and we thought it might be the last.
and in case our grandkids ask,
"were you ever young?"
we want to prove
we were someone
who did things
and didn't just languish
in a fake waiting room.

DANILO MACHADO

I grew up witnessing my parents' directional fluency from the passenger seat, but it was only later that I connected it to our experience of migration and undocumentedness. In retrospect, the carefulness of their driving was understandable, especially as they spent many years not being able to obtain a license. To this day, even after status adjustment, I still don't have my license or know how to drive, partially a holdover from pre-DACA teenage anxieties.

With or without the ability to "return," migration forces distancing from home; fading memories as time away accumulates. It is part of the violence that is both felt and countered in the everyday. Unassuming moments—unfolding road maps, telling stories in living rooms—hold significant diasporic loss only implied by the language of policy, but also represent a counterimagining to the state's policing of movement. How is navigation protest? What does it mean to border-cross by remembering cartographies of home and, in turn, reclaim permission?

The so-called United States not only does not see, respect, or protect most of its migrants, but carries a history of stolen land and labor. In this context, the poem contends with how, as uninvited guests, we can still make our being "well-located" reject colonial entitlement.

In the end, considering these experiences has become instructional like maps are. My thoughts and this poem have been as evolving and incomplete as them, too. They have illuminated connections not just in my own intimate family but made clear the structural forces that we've been shaped by and the grief, frustration, and possibility that they carry.

mapping/s

the map in my dashboard
is outdated and missing
two states, my left arm browned
from hanging out the car window

—Solmaz Sharif[6]

/ even now,
        i see you
    diagonally

from my seat
    in the ford explorer
as dad drives

    and you unfold
creased aaa maps
    kept tucked beside you,

    highlighted highways and detours
matte collections of drivable distances
    supplemented by glossy guidebooks,

direct swifter than
    the electronic navigator's
loud overlapping interjections

            what does it mean to be well
located in land that's not yours
            twice over?

to come to soil
(also colonized)
and become fluent
in its jumbled,
made-up language
and built roads?

does it protect you?

is it a comfort?
does it remind you of how much
you've had to learn

to navigate

traffic tolls, laws
permissions, il
legalities

//
i joke often that the skill
for mapping and direction
(which even my brother has)

skipped me
and this
has become fitting:

because queerness
has shown itself to be a set of
disorientations

HERE TO STAY

///

        in living room conversations
           with your friends
        (many granted
    permission to return)

you recount places
    inaccessible
        for now

travel to them
        by naming
: locating   landmarks,
        neighborhoods

    —those conjured cardinals of medellín
i can't follow
    become lost reminders

    of what i don't know
        of the roads that wouldn't
recognize me
    upon return

BEATRIZ YANES MARTINEZ

I wrote my first poem in second grade—years before I was rendered illegal the moment I crossed the Rio Grande. I chose to continue to write, then as a way to let out that teenage angst, as a way to assert agency, and because I wanted to be a singer/songwriter at some point, but I didn't exactly have the voice for it; I chose to write to defy my father who didn't think I could become a writer; I chose to write as I made sense and continue to make sense of myself as a queer person, I chose to write because it brings me joy and that is enough. I don't write poetry because I am undocumented. I am undocumented and I write poetry. And as I write this statement, I reflect on what it means to be an undocumented person—and how insufficient, how misleading that word often feels to describe us. We've been rendered illegal by the state—many of us, in a state of hyperdocumentation.

And it is in this continued assertion against illegality that is forced upon my body where some of my poetry has taken me. How can my body, and by extension, my writing, become not only an altar of unforgetting, but also a portal for healing? What am I doing to continuously reject embodied colonial and state violence? How does my writing function as a form of refusal? And how can I begin to dream (outside of the American construction of Dreaming, outside of the Dreamer narrative) of the past, present, and into the future? These are questions I ask—and I am still searching for answers.

Cyborg

Echoes of ochre contour into residue of abandonment. I grew a third skin: umber labyrinths packaged as cans of mildewed impatience. It was the pieces of ash from another burning of caña fields falling like a rainstorm that reminded me I have a ritual to complete.

Date of Journal: Yesterday
I extracted a red anemone from the roots in my head that had haunted me but instead I uprooted my trauma. The almanac tells me to cultivate it during moonscapes, use indigo and ash to grow it into an antenna.

Date of Journal: Tomorrow
I wait for the eggs to morph into nymphs. This is the long wait. I document or whatever. I enter my own instar. I dream of growing wings. I dream of becoming a ship. I dream of learning to fly.

I wake up.

Date of Journal: It's always the afternoon thunderstorms—when the petrichor alters itself into a memory.
I walk barefoot collecting cicadas' second skins. I grow sketches of their armor. Dream blueprint studies of their exoskeleton after the molting. I use a magnifying glass to trace the maps contoured onto their transparent wings. I wait.

Date of Journal: I wait. I wait.

Date of Journal: Madrugada.
When the anemone membranes itself into the antenna, the cicada's stridulation transforms itself into a compass. I checked two things off from my list: map, and compass. The cacophony permanents itself in my head. My body becomes nocturnal.

Date of Journal: I wait.
The cicadas enter their next long sleep. I memorize the route.

Date of Journal: The time when the sun glistens in the forest like honey, like lava.
Or the time is running out. Instar is defined as the stage in the life of the arthropod between two successive molts (ecdysis).

Date of Journal: Sometime, yesterday.
I designed my space suit from mantas y rayos de sol. Elytra wings made out of the petals from the anemone, the leaves from the last plantain tree in my grandparents' garden. I build a kite with stems of dried-up coconut leaves, yesterday's newspapers and thread from mami's sewing kit.

One day, I grew wings. One day, I became a ship.

Date of Journal: One day.
I learned to fly.

This poem sits atop a displaced chimeric volcano

And a mangrove written over in the footnotes
The question always searches for a past
When do we go back? I look for the ephemeral puddles
after the thunderstorms and read them like coffee grounds
Distorted mirrored oscillations but at least the petrichor
is an intravenous memory that injects me with an ellipsis
I gather buckets of salt water to create a centrifuge
Para desterrar a metaphor that lives inside my throat
I look for the crescent moon above Ilopango
and trace you a memory onto your flesh and ask you:
Where does this illegalized queer body erupt to their full glory?
I once read that Ilopango's ashes could be found all the way in Antarctica
What I mean to say is, we're still searching for that place where we once belonged.

YESSICA MARTINEZ

This poem is part of a manuscript titled *Aircraft*. As a child migrant and DACA status holder, I consider in *Aircraft* what it is to have the ground taken from underneath one's feet; to be lifted and left suspended in an up-in-the-air space where all landings and returns are deferred. In this poem, however, I am not violently lifted, but am instead embraced at ground level by my father after a three-year separation. Here, I am not in transit, there are no aircraft or other vehicles of flight forced upon me. Rather it is language that as a craft of air envelops the environment around us, creating a swirling storm that diffuses our surroundings, foregrounds our embrace, and earnestly folds us into each other. There is an erotic of belonging in this poem. I refer to the erotic as Audre Lorde describes it in "Uses of the Erotic": in contrast to the abused and the pornographic, as more than and not exclusive to the sexual realm, as a primordial life force and rhythm through which one's sense of self is both intensified and bewildered.[7] Here, tenderness supersedes the frontier of the self as my father and I mirror each other and morph into other mammalian bodies to be brought primally close. We are warm-blooded, instinctually territorial. My father's protective drive—the same instinct that paradoxically pushed him to leave us and migrate—is allowed to briefly reconcile itself in this embrace. Reunited, we are of the ground, each other's gravity.

Mammalian Longing

I land in 2003 and my father picks me up - no - he bends to his knees - and my
escort disappears - the snowstorm - enters John Efe airport - and takes the rest

in a flurry - not even my mother is there - though she insists - my father and I
swear - it is only my father and I - his red hot ears - in the plumpness

of our coats - his North Face and the one he cloaks - over my leather
matching - I am his cub - I am his deer - his piglet and he - all babas and teeth

bites hoof - poof marks - into my cheek - this is the most - we've been in love
since.

FARID MATUK

I was thinking of Etel Adnan's *Arab Apocalypse*. The poem reveals its own depth inside a wellspring of life, at once a beyond and a source of categories and of any judgments they could inspire.

"We speak and compose in the reanimated forms of others so that linguistic expression is the historical resurgence of alterity," Lisa Robertson says. I love that. It reframes private language (the lyric?) and any interiority found there as communal, disbursed.

I was thinking of my scrolling through videos, looking for intimacies that never wanted to be private.

In "Mama's Baby, Papa's Maybe," Hortense Spillers theorizes "flesh," a zero-degree of embodiment to which enslaved peoples are consigned, a register prior to gender or subjectivity or any other nicety of civil society. The essay's subtitle is "An American Grammar Book."

I was thinking how I was preemptively kidnapped at six and brought to the U.S., my mother running from my father. My father's brother was in charge of Lima's police, so we were running from the Janus head of patriarchy and the state. We lived undocumented until the retroactive amnesty of 1987.

Anyone could try to get a passport, but we believe in being documentable because we are non-Black. Conditionally assimilable to the state, we don't sink into flesh.

Event: a happening, also an outcome, from Latin *eventus*, from e-, "out of," + venire, "come." I want the impossibility: to leave from any means of arriving.

Whiteness is a reaching for property and capital, for dominion as a cosmology under which one narrows into a "one," for a militarized state to defend that diminishment, to promise such in a document. I sometimes mistake for intimacy the frenzy of whiteness in its self-reactions, its unacknowledged attempts to fall down from document back into flesh.

Without being glib about the conditional and unevenly distributed protections of civil society, Claudia Rankine writes, "Join me down here in nowhere."

The document has only altitude, from which it drops us back down to our event—to fall back into leaving, vacating detachment, rightly, unwelcomed in the words.

I was thinking of just saying it: love me and don't believe in me.

Video Tryouts for an American Grammar Book

There is no backward. A turn of wind through the window at the spider's filaments.

A mirror, turned, a plow, an eager representative of technology.

The trees, lined stalls of private homes, a romance of staying in place. Light at my thumb, lemon yellow line. What searching I've sent.

A speckled bird swoops between the legs of two people in a video to seize the dead prairie dog from the fist of its keeper.

The bird flies in a video it mistakes for another time. The bird has already threshed audience from the real people who understand.

Sun letting the fog pass by. The audience that marvels feels left behind in its own outline. The idea of a word realized as audience to that distance.

In this yellow light I'm glad for the sentence dropping off from the surface. A video of soldiers wailing after scenes of them sleeping.

My eyes closing and my belief in interiority I've come to drop off. In their sleeping, their mouths agog. A different video of boys spitting tobacco into each other's mouths.

The depth from which. A man in a video giving his gut and face to be punched. A video of fields smoking or a video of the mown grasses? A video of a man sucking another's cock by an ATV. Their long beards orphaned into objects.

Voyage to the surface of sleep the soldiers seem to go to   a waking video
a sleeping video   expected all the way into its genre.

A painted video   carries the squeak of boats lurching at their moorings.   A video orphans the voice Etel gives to reading her poems, a critic returns it.

A video of a man's rectum bleeding fast from the mason jar that just broke inside his full feeling.

A video made sacred by the last seven videos.

            A video of the bleeding or a video of what happened
after his hand reaches to stop the recording. A mistake that sees the flesh the body tries to run from.

Men sleeping placid beneath the river looking up with both eyes dedicated
to the patriarchy is the cardboard sleeve

cover image for a video of men congratulating men
for writing about the ugliness of men.

Boots in near unison, an uncomplicated feeling in a video of me tucked into a low-back stretch looking up at the plastered ceiling   humming a singer's dead American voice—*that's on me . . . that's on me . . . I know . . .*

        far from people on a mesa getting closer to the sun
by looking out to the reservoir evaporating in a line at the sun.

Refrigeration, ornithology, benediction   earnest, mimicking
a closed set of faces. A video of a U.S. fighter pilot and I at the Delta Airlines gate, his enthusiasm shining   as far as the air will take it.

A video of me hearing him say, God's work   for where his enthusiasm meets his enthusiasm for the mission

                            so his smiling can go inside himself

in a video of him showing me his flight helmet and oxygen mask I am seeing him
holding his own head in his lap   before it goes back in his monogrammed
duffel bag.

He has only altitude and the promise of an executioner renouncing hierarchies
a video they think they make but I think it.   My thinking worn away with its single
eye knocked loose so it rolls inward is a name.

A video of me being used to consent to the conditions.   Soft mole, hale tunnels,
standing house.   I narrow into a fine, stretchable line, thin blue, a bright yellow
edge of least depth, the sound of its going.

Down the hall. A door creaking in a video about the importance of sequencing
begins, Down the hall, so the door will have somewhere to sound, hesitant

               or grand, opening onto the bank of the river
marking an edge to the Motherland of objects, reposed, frayed, remembered in
museums, you first

                                        the water's still fine. A technology of
staying, not of staying in place. There is a feeling that I like when you love me
and don't believe in me, even as a sentence has only altitude
from which it falls   back toward its event.

ALINE MELLO

I cannot separate my work from my undocumented identity. Maybe I wouldn't even be a poet if I were not undocumented. In another life, maybe I'm just writing steamy romance novels. My being undocumented isn't just a phase or a minor identity marker. Sociologist Everett Hughes coined the phrase "master status" to name a primary identity that affects every aspect of one's life and determines their future trajectory. My immigration status is my master status because it has and does and will affect every aspect of my life. Think of it as prescription glasses. I have been wearing them since I was five years old, but sometimes I forget I even have them on. Have you ever forgotten you were wearing your glasses? Or maybe you were on a roller coaster and after you were strapped in, remembered your glasses, then had to decide if you should take them off or keep them on? And do you ever go awhile without thinking of your eyesight, then get that yearly reminder that it's time to get it checked? This is the undocumented status: always there, sometimes more obviously so, sometimes discreetly. I wonder about the indent my status will leave on my body, long after it changes, or after I leave, not unlike how the weight of the glasses presses down on your nose, reshaping it. But the voice in my poems lives in her other identities as well: a woman in a bigger body, a Brazilian who is disconnected from her native country, a dog person. I hope the voice in my poems is able to show that undocumented people get to be party girls or divorcées or health nuts or class clowns or chronically ill or serial daters or all of it all at once. My poetry is constantly aware of displacement and the inhumane ways we treat each other because of a made-up thing like citizenship. I hope my poems are political. I hope my poems are disruptive. I hope my poems reach for the reader to say, *I know, I see it too*, or, *Do you know? Do you see it?*

Between Americas

The military dictatorship ended
the year my sister was born

but we were too poor to notice.
The president talked about

sustaining erections on September 7th
and kissed his young wife

and said he's not a rapist but
if he were, he'd go only

for the pretty ones. He's selective.
Unlike Molly my dog, who barks at everyone—

children, women, UFOs, little boys taking
turns on training wheels.

She barks because they're outside
and she is not

and she is too.
You see, power has to be wrenched.

There are always little revolutions—
like how a group of ants can topple

down a grasshopper surely,
and how my mom's medium-sized

HERE TO STAY

feet, chicken breast feet,
took her from one part of Spain

to another while she carried a picture
of one of my dead uncles.

I like to press down on the veins.
The revolution we need

next week is a literal one
with maybe violence and maybe wars.

We will need a year after just to breathe
then another to pull up the pipes,

fill in the mines, the way we have carved
ourselves into the earth

when maybe we shouldn't have?
What I mean to say is, in class

a Sociology PhD student asked
if DACA came with financial aid

and when I said no, she said she couldn't
imagine how any undocumented person

could ever get an education.
And yesterday the 5th circuit courts

declared DACA illegal. And I am
more tired than I was last week.

I never asked for DACA.
The truth is, tomorrow there's another

hurricane with another name
and America is still America is still America.

Family Keepsake

My grandmother wanted to die
but in the online form, I say *no,*

no family member has died by
or attempted suicide
because

having children,
no matter the goal,
is still giving life. Because

that's what blood is.
The psychiatrist asked
if she'd tried to kill herself before.
I said *seven times.* Success on the 8th

child. But I want to say that
my grandfather was good to her.
She loved her children. She gave

again and again and
maybe, this time, it was her turn
to keep herself to herself.

Trying Not to Think of My Grandmother's Grave

Cemetery under mud,
rain deciding for me—
like my parents did
like the laws do—
deciding I'd never visit.
I want to give her daisies,
margaridas like her name,
and pretend
just a little
like I usually do
that what
connects us
is more than blood,
but what is true
is that she's
buried
then buried again.

One day,
if I go back
I will
walk by the rivers
that are prone to flooding
barefoot, hoping,
careful,
not to kick my grandmother
with my toes
but maybe run into her
casually
like one runs into family

HERE TO STAY

shopping for shoes
at the store,
to say bença vó
press my cheek to hers,
dig two holes into wet earth
sink my arms into them,
like gloves made of mud,
the closest I'll get
to an embrace.

MARIA CAROLINA
MURRIEL TOLEDO

Years ago, I left my friends and family in Miami to go puff up my career in Boston. Lonely, I went to therapy consistently and resolved to distance myself from my father. I felt revulsion for his hot temper, scathing tantrums, and overdrinking—more than anything because I had emulated them for so long and was struggling to stop.

Burnt out, I quit the big job I'd moved there for and decided I would make art as a rebellion. I would not care about money, career, making my parents proud. I would stay unemployed indefinitely. I would be a person not consumed by necessity, but propelled by desire.

I thought this was a further distancing from my father, but in my every endeavor he appeared to me. When I looked at myself, I found him in my reflection. How was my artist's rebellion different from his pursuit of the American Dream? My father, the self-taught builder, the driver of our migration, the big dreamer who fed us from trades he learned through the force of his will?

This poem is the raw acknowledgment that when I look into my heart, I find my father in every corner. Tucked away behind my dreams, my drive, my curiosity. My inspiration.

Taking Up Woodworking

The wood splintered on my shirt and I smelled musty. Like a mouth that's been closed for too long.

As I shook my gray top free of sawdust and tree pieces I felt like my father.
I'd seen him like this. Gray v-neck, thick denim, steel-toed boots. Sweating through his t-shirt. Dripping from his brow.
Rings of dirt cradling his neck.

I was my father here.
Dirty, tired, musty, saw.

Though I could never be that workhorse. I drank too much last night and I already need a nap.
But I'm trying to power. Picking up the scraps of wood that will help me reach the pit of my nostalgia.

The pain this wood might cause my palms and fingers. The sting my eyes might feel when I crack open its dust. The salt my mouth will taste when I can only produce tears.

Forget using this for art. All I can create is sadness.
Saws and dust and sweat and sad. Woods and would'ves.
Panicked gasping in the nighttime. Words we choked on in the past.

I've become my father now.
Wild and angry and pure and strong. Splintered and oxidic. Radioactive.
Proven wrong.

JOSÉ OLIVAREZ

"Ars Poetica" began as a statement of poetics for a grant I was applying to. The grant asked for an "introduction to your work." That exercise felt tedious, so I began, instead, where all my poems begin: with migration. When I wrote, "Plot twist: migration never ends," it felt like I had revealed something fundamentally true about my life, my family, and my writing. Migration didn't end when my parents arrived undocumented in the United States in the 1980s. It didn't end when my dad passed his citizenship test eleven years later. No, every year I learn something new about what migration cost my family: the relatives whose birthdays we missed: who are now buried where all my ancestors are buried: whose funerals we could not attend. Every week someone asks me where I'm from: no, where I'm really from. And if I said, "Chicago," do you think I could ever really claim it?

ARS POETICA

Migration is derived from the word "migrate," which is a verb defined by Merriam-Webster as "to move from one country, place, or locality to another." Plot twist: migration never ends. My parents moved from Jalisco, México, to Chicago in 1987. They were dislocated from México by capitalism, and they arrived in Chicago just in time to be dislocated by capitalism. Question: is migration possible if there is no "other" land to arrive in. My work: to imagine. My family started migrating in 1987 and they never stopped. I was born mid-migration. I've made my home in that motion. Let me try again: I tried to become American, but America is toxic. I tried to become Mexican, but México is toxic. My work: to do more than reproduce the toxic stories I inherited and learned. In other words: just because it is art doesn't mean it is inherently nonviolent. My work: to write poems that make my people feel safe, seen, or otherwise loved. My work: to make my enemies feel afraid, angry, or otherwise ignored. My people: my people. My enemies: capitalism. Susan Sontag: "victims are interested in the representation of their own sufferings." Remix: survivors are interested in the representation of their own survival. My work: survival. Question: Why poems? Answer: ▮▮▮▮▮

Middle Class in This Mf

(by Pedro Olivarez Jr., via text message to José Olivarez)

Bro, I'm getting recruitment emails from companies tryna hire the kid

I'm bout to be MIDDLE CLASS in this mf

Finna get my teeth straightened boiiii

Finna get regular check ups at the doctor boiiiii

Finna get a new prescription and new glasses and new contacts boiiii

You ain't never seen nobody be middle class like me before. I'm gonna crush it bro. Mid level sedan, decent watch, dress shoes, buttoned up gas tank half full

MARIA D. DUARTE ORTIZ

Until dawn I understood the breaking of oneself into little pieces of debris flying from one city to the next—never stopping—never settling for one place. In the forest of my mind, I am flying into the depths of my being where I can find the tree of life shedding petals to cover the floor. I can never see the floor, I don't know if it's covered in wood or carpet or just cement—the floor always escapes my reach and by the time I aim to tackle the question of, am I ever going to belong? The night comes to hide me. The face I was is no more. I do not know how to be the people that I am.

It's okay if I cannot go to Paris, but is it? Why think about it when it can't happen? My life isn't as bad, I am not dying or starving, I have a roof over my head and a job, the surviving is there. But it feels like a disaster.

Fingernails

Their creation known to men
as a myth. The moon came looking
for a witness of her illumination on earth
and found that she could not fit whole
in the wrinkles of our faces,
so we carry her in our working hands
as a crescent almost invisible to our eyes.

JANEL PINEDA

I write as the U.S.-born daughter of Zenayda and Omar, each of whom migrated undocumented to Los Angeles at the onset of the U.S.-funded Salvadoran Civil War in 1980. My family's experiences of continuous and varying forms of displacement have shaped my poetic practice into one that envisions new possibilities for what it can mean to build "home" when "home" is an unstable, shifting place. How might we dream and organize toward a world where home is never threatened, where safety and human rights are not conditional?

"In Another Life" imagines a world without borders, without the state violences that have forced many, including my family, to leave their homes and seek refuge elsewhere. In the poem, I wrestle with historical memory, familial stories, and abolitionist politics to honor the "alternate world" that is made possible through the collective care of family members present throughout the poem. War, hunger, violence, are replaced by abundance. Throughout "In Another Life," a mother's love, a grandmother's stories, a community mercado of frutas, wins.

"Feeding Finches" and "The Yellow Jackets" grapple with a different kind of loss, a different sort of displacement: the loss of a physical home that embodies decades of sacrifice and struggle. In my family, there was no dream of a white picket fence—but there was always the dream of a home where everyone could gather, where everyone was welcome. At the heart of these two poems is my father, a custodian of the natural world; his tenderness with finches and roses take center stage. These poems honor the interconnectedness of our human strife for survival and the persistence of the natural world around us. So the finches will be fed, so the yellow jackets will take shelter, so a family can keep a roof over their heads.

Feeding Finches

Ever since the foreclosure notice was
posted on our front door, my father has
been feeding finches. Palming safflower
seeds and shelled corn and white proso millet
into a makeshift feeder by my sister's
plants. The finches come in flocks, bowing
before food. My father watches them take
turns wing-bathing in the dog bowl before
flying off. He lets them go, knowing they'll
return, knowing he'll feed them again.
What else is a man's worth, but the promise
of seeds he offers his children? What else
but the halo of a roof he secures
atop their heads?

The Yellow Jackets

When they began nesting on the eaves of our home
the summer we were almost without one
I couldn't find it in me to do anything
but watch one after the other, drifting
determinedly toward our roof.

They spent July busying themselves
with my father's roses, picking
at caterpillars, taking refuge from the heat.
I watched their queen carry half her weight
in chewed-up wood, then use it to build
her hiding place on my porch.

Something tells me I should have gotten rid of them,
but what sense did it make? To rid myself
of what I could live peacefully beside?
To take their home while we begged to be
allowed to keep ours?

In Another Life

The war never happened but somehow you and I
        still exist. Like obsidian,
we know only the memory of lava
        and not the explosion that created

us. Forget the gunned-down church, the burning
        flesh, the cabbage soup.
There is no bus. There is no border. There is no blood.
        There are

only sweet corn fields and mango skins. The turquoise
        house and clotheslines.
A heaping plate of pasteles and curtido waiting to be
        disappeared into our bellies.

In this life, our people are not things of silences
        but whole worlds bursting
into breath. Everywhere, there are children. Playing
        freely, clothed and clean.

Mozote does not mean massacre and flowers bloom
        in every place shoes are
left behind. My name still means truth, this time
        in a language my mouth recognizes,

in a language I know how to speak. My grandmother is
        still a storyteller although I am
not a poet. In this life, I do not have to be. This poem
        somehow still exists. It is told

in my mother's voice and she makes hurt dissolve like honey
    in hot water, manzanilla
warming the throat. You and I do not find each other
    on another continent, grasping

at each other's necks in search of home. We meet in a mercado,
    my arms overflowing
with mamey and anonas, and together we wash them
    in riverwater. We watch sunset fall over

a land we call our own and do not fear its taking.
    I bite into the fruit, mouth sucking
seed from substance, pulling its veins from between my teeth.
    Our laughter echoes

from inside the cave, one we are free to step outside of.
    We do not have to hide here.
We do not have to hide anywhere. A torogoz flies past my face
    and I do not fear its flapping.

JORGE QUINTANA

I am undocumented.

And in a sentence, a lifetime of trauma opens. The sand that swallows children in the desert of northern Mexico is at my feet, so my work is an attempt to describe the feeling of drowning in a place absent of water. "Lunada" is the product of immigration, of being from a place but not belonging to it. The closest I get to the Mexico I was born in is through my parents. I was not raised in Mexico, but my mother's laughter was, which means my laughter was. So when I laugh, this means I have a home somewhere. I am obsessed with connection. I see myself as a part of all things, which often informs my work and the way it rambles. One line becomes the next and there is no distinction where one ends and the other begins. This manifests in "The poem where ants are immigrants and I am the U.S.," a poem where two narratives interrupt one another. One is a monologue of killing ants, the other is a textual rationalization of it. Both narratives stagger across the page in search of definition. In the United States all things are defined and categorized, especially people. So when I attempt to describe/define what being undocumented feels like there is both the emotional and the systemic. What I am and what I am. The body I inhabit and the number it is missing to prove it exists.

The poem where ants are immigrants and I am the U.S.

sometimes when I kill ants I feel guilty
because I'm an immigrant yet I feel justified to
pass mortal judgment on those I consider
trespassers in my home

> [home is a metaphor for country //
> immigrant is a metaphor for invisibility
> that is inherited]

but I can't blame them for being hungry
for looking for food and finding it
in our cupboards, it's no body's fault
that there's abundance here

> [hunger is a loose translation for the desire
> for citizenship // in my dreams I see ants
> crossing deserts for sustenance but finding
> death at my hand]

but it's hard to ignore them because
where there's one ant there's an entire
fucking colony

> [colony is a metaphor for the way all my
> cousins and I fit perfectly together in one
> bed]

so I have to kill the ants,
if I let them stay they'll only spread
so I murder them instead
and that's the way the world is sometimes
just because we wait in line to eat
doesn't mean we will actually get to

[eating is a sacred act that my ancestors
sacrificed for // to fill my belly with food
is to survive my own mortality]

I remember waiting in line with
my mom to get WIC food stamps
and the new cereals we got to buy
and the ants that noticed
and devoured them before I could
but even then I couldn't blame the ants
for being tired of our poverty
and rejoicing in something new

[poverty is my way of describing the lack
of sugar variety in our cereal boxes // I
still remember the first time my dad
brought home Frosted Flakes instead of
Corn Flakes]

but even though I don't blame them
I still kill them whenever they
begin to hoard in our home

[home is still a metaphor for country]

some I drown
some I stomp on
some I allow to escape
as my form of mercy

[mercy is a metaphor for asylum //
the only way we can distinguish between
the foolish and the lucky]

but in the end
they always come back

in more numbers
no matter how many ants I kill
they still come back looking
for food even though they
only find death
maybe what makes
a colony a colony is the
refusal to die (completely)

[death can only be a metaphor for itself //
food is still sacred // a colony is still my
cousins and I piled up on each other //
laughing instead of sleeping]

and I don't blame the ants
for wanting to survive
their winter even if
if it means dying at
my boot

[winter is a metaphor for U.S. interventions
in Latin America]

I don't blame them
for the way they live
I even pray for them
as they die
I pray that their next lives
are filled with less mercy
and more sovereignty
I pray that we never cross paths again
and if we do I just hope that
they show me the same kindness

[sovereignty is a dream I inherited from my
father // prayers are the way we show

love to the dead // the way we show them
we still remember who they were before
they left home]

and if they don't
how could I blame them
when on my conscience
I carry the murder of
entire colonies

God dear God,
will I be forgiven for all the ants I've killed?

Lunada

Happiness is a shade of my mother's laughter. It echoes in my chest. I believe wholeheartedly in the genetics of emotion. So when entire oceans pour out of me, I recognize my ancestors in the water.

There is nothing I can't swallow whole. I'm afraid of drowning in my own mouth. It's what I inherited from the men in my family. We are thirsty for land and find echoes of ourselves in the calls of the birds. My body is the origin story of Icarus. My hands are myth. Everything I touch is swallowed by the dirt. And I belong to the soil anyway.

It's the first thing I inherited from my father. I couldn't inherit his homeland. His Mexico is a laughter that doesn't fit inside my diaphragm. I am a man of many voices. They cascade into horizons. They empty me. They set with the sun and call for the moon. They are the gravity at my ankles. The jokes whispered by the wind.

There are times I forget how to laugh. How to turn the cosmic into comedy. How to let my feet sink into the moment, for a moment. Sometimes I'm afraid I'll look at the moon for the last time and not know it. Is there an emotion older than fear? Older than hate?

Is there laughter that doesn't fade? That buries itself into the ground like arsenic. That sticks to the sky like the oxygen living in my lungs.

YOSIMAR REYES

I have no control over my undocumented predicament, there is nothing I can do to change this. At thirty-five years old I have realized that beyond its legalities, being undocumented is a spiritual and emotional warfare. Undocumentedness and the messaging around it is a project that polices the imagination.

I wrote "Undocumented Joy" because I was simply tired of having to re-count my lived experience to pursue "the moveable middle." I grew tired of the pressure to plead my case to citizens who are often too ignorant to understand their own immigration system and yet feel confident enough to ask me, "Why don't you do it the right way?"

I had to rid myself of this and go inward. I made the choice to have my writing be an ointment, a prayer, a word of encouragement to the people who that is the most. In the fight for immigrant rights, the people who I have lost the most have been us, the undocumented.

My poetry is a reminder to us that we have given so much; now it's time we protect our energy, our spirits, our joy. We cannot let this country take away our ability to smile. These poems are for you who are tired. You do not have to explain anything to me, I get it, I see you and I believe in you.

There is nothing beautiful about being undocumented, but if I must find something, it is that we found each other with our voices.

Illegal

Everyone knows that en el Apartamento 26
you can get your "green card"

There in that two-bedroom apartment
you can become American

write your name and birthday on a piece of paper
and come out with your social

There in this torn-down apartment building
dreams come true

Here in this abandoned place
with these forgotten people,
we became "legal."
by our own laws

Undocumented Joy

I don't remember crossing

so I cannot tell you about the journey

sometimes I close my eyes and imagine a pitch-

black sky with a thousand little stars

imagine a poetic crossing

my Abuela's hand tugging at my arm a rush of wind

Abuelo leading the way

I imagine crossing without fear

just dreams

and Abuela's goals

to raise my brother and me

into hardworking men

I crossed without the trauma latching unto my body

crossed unscarred

mis viejitos

HERE TO STAY

tell me

how they had to

stuff the four of us under the backseat of a car

sometimes I wish I could remember then maybe just maybe

I would have another story to tell

I can only tell you about how poor we were living in that small apartment

in the Eastside

how embarrassed I was

to invite my friends over

even though we all lived like this

I can only tell you how proud I was of Abuela who asked me to teach her English

scribbled on the refrigerator door

you can sometimes see the residue

of the markers used to teach her basic words

like thank you, God bless you & you are welcome

I wish you would ask about the memories

I had before my identity became political

about the laughs

the joy

the things I love

about the way I have managed to survive

I wish you would focus on the magic that is to take the world's trash

and make it into art

I wish I could tell you about the journey but all I know is that I am here

I'm not going anywhere

this is my home

now.

Why Don't You Just Get Married?

I don't want to *have to* marry a citizen

I want the day I fall in love
to be without me thinking nation
and allegiance

want it to be how the white girls
in the movies do it
carelessly
running through the streets of New York City
fucking everybody until
I meet a man that meets all my feminist ideals

I want the day I fall in love
to be without me thinking
if he has a social
if he can keep me here

I don't want the pressure of thinking
that after 30 years of living here
he is a blessing
an opening
a crack
in the system
for me to get in

I don't want to think of green cards, visas
of finally having a foundation to step on

I want my loving to be an option
not a way out of my condition

I want the day
I set foot on the altar
gaze into his eyes

be the day I know
papers don't matter
But betch, papers would be nice tho.

CATALINA RIOS

In American culture when someone dies we see the relationship we had with them as an ending. But what if you never had the opportunity to say goodbye, or carry the weight of knowing that even through death, you have to worry about belonging in a land where you will be laid to "rest." In these poems, I reclaim my relationship to my ancestors through curiosity to find belonging. I also critique the ways in which empire has determined how we say goodbye to our loved ones; how borders do not allow us to rest and heal our wounds of displacement.

Burial While Undocumented

The cloudy day did not stop
us from honoring our dead
with a picnic.
As we turn the corner
from the road construction
that never seems to end,
there's a celebration of
life; miles long of fighting
for memories to stay.
She heard this from someone—
you know the *she said* stories—
and asked:
can undocumented people
be buried *here*?
but, she really meant to ask:
will *I* have a place to rest?

Abuela Catalina

Using a line from "Shoulda Been Jimi Savannah" by Patricia Smith

I have so many questions. What chair did you use to rest your arm
after a long day of scrubbing clothes clean? How did you say goodbye to each
of your children as you lost them to immigration? How did your lips move with
    each syllable
as you pronounced our name? There are pictures of you. Your hair touched by
    midnight with waves and coils too steadfast to pin. Your son named me after
    you. His tiny
daughter inherited your nose, the fuzzy vision, and a heart armed with benign
    weaponry.
Your son once told me he chased you as you left to care for wealthy people's
    children, so
fast he lost his way home. Years later he filled that hole with the liquid that
    numbs. No
one could bring him back from the rejection his limbs breathed. What was the
    one
joke that made you giggle like a schoolgirl? Forgetting the poverty that would
eventually call your spirit home. How did all the storm of lies and mistake
-s of men feel in your belly, and of your children? I thought it was only me
who saw through the facade of lightly sprinkled promises to keep us in place for
longer than we intended. But luckily, I also inherited your Iris, telling the gods
    anything
to stay afloat through the rough winds, traveling into the depths of the sea as
    they tried to other
us into submission. What color was your skin in the Spring of 1964? Was it
    browner than
the soil I rarely remember the tips of my fingers caressing? Did you feel the
    rejection of a government not caring enough for its people? Allowing them
    to swim and drink from tricky waters. Being the goddess of the rainbow did
    very little in this land, but you are now a whisperer

reminding the living to be like waves when it's time to leave. What did you carry with

you in your purse when you walked to the market to buy the ingredients for the recipe of a

new day? Was it hope to find the juiciest guayabas, or a wooden handle switchblade

ready to grasp between your fingers when your instincts tell you it's time? How many times in

a day did you look in the mirror to see the reflection of your mother? When my father told me I

have his eyes, that's all I pray to see from now on, even with weights in my shoe.

JORGE MENA ROBLES

On my way home to Chicago, after traveling to Mexico City and Guadalajara in 2015, I presented my Advance Parole documents to Department of Homeland Security officials at Dulles International Airport. Twenty years after my original departure from Mexico, I had traveled to Mexico City as part of the "Youth Without Borders" [Jovenes Sin Fronteras] convening that brought together youth from throughout North America to share their experiences and to strategize and build a transnational organizing network. During that trip, I reunited with family in Guadalajara that I had not seen since third grade.

As I sat in the second inspection room waiting for my name to be called by the officers, I witnessed the interactions between them and recently arrived migrants. It was explicit that there was no room for disobedience. Officials held the ability to deny me (and others) entry to the country where my mother, sister, and I had lived for most of my life. My ability to reenter the US—this time legally—was in their hands. One officer made their authority clear by saying "Don't be causing anyone any trouble—especially when you're an illegal" before letting me go on my way. This poem serves as both testament and witness to what migrants (even those with a modicum of protection via DACA) must endure while "legally" crossing borders.

User Guide

Advance Parole Travels (JULY 21, 2015):

Arrive in Washington DC at 3:30 pm from CDMX.
The whole process with CBP will take 2 hours.

The first check-in is relatively quick. You will wait in line for 33 minutes. It will feel longer.

The first CBP agent, an Asian woman, will check your passport, take your fingerprints, and point you to the next office. First inspection.

Walk into the office and hand your documents to the second agent (passport, both AP copies) & take a seat.

In front of you, an agent will then begin to question an older gentleman who has been an LPR for 47 years as to why he has not become a U.S. citizen. Remain seated.

There will be about 15 other strangers in the room when he says this.

The agent will then remind the gentleman that he has a DUI and that he's a "guest" in this country. They will let him go on his way after this warning.

After waiting in this second room for 55 minutes, you will miss your connecting flight.

A different agent will now tell a different gentleman that he has presented the wrong visa and that he can only stay 2 more months, legally, in the U.S. The agent will tell the señor that he knows he wasn't trying to stay here to work illegally and that he should go find answers at his embassy. They let him go.

HERE TO STAY

After almost two hours in customs, a young Latino agent will call you up.

"Where are you headed to?"
(Chicago)

"What happened in 2011?"
(Civil disobedience, found not guilty)

Sit back down.
Called back up.

"What do you do?"
(Student)

"Don't be causing anyone any trouble. Especially when you're an illegal."

Wait for him to stamp your passport. To stamp the AP form. Agent will keep one of the two copies. He won't ask why you traveled. He doesn't care.

They let you go.

LETICIA PRIEBE ROCHA

Poetry is an art of acute observation and listening. These skills blossomed within me naturally from childhood, and I strive to nurture them as an adult, though there is a heaviness inherent to that level of sensitivity that can be difficult to carry. Like many who experience migration, trauma, and their intersections, I often struggle to feel grounded physically, mentally, spiritually. In the moments where I slip from my personhood, words have been the most consistent anchors back to myself. I move about the world collecting how we attempt (and often fail) to communicate with each other, then process these exchanges and articulate the voices that shape me on the page. Incorporating dialogue in my work serves as a tribute to our inherent interconnectedness. For me, the sonnet form has been particularly fruitful in this endeavor because it evokes a sense of urgency that gives way to my bravest, most vulnerable voice. The constraint of fourteen lines mirrors the ephemeral nature of our time on this earth. Holding the reality of this one precious life necessitates that every turn of phrase becomes a revelation, a celebration, a love letter to feeling, to being alive, and the journey toward our most radiant selves.

Alignment

I.

I was five or six, one of those tender ages where absolutely nothing made sense
and I was okay with it. A girl in my class made spitting remarks and I spit back.
The teacher told us to be good, make nice, apologize. Grown-ups were always right,
so I said my sorrys. Something about it hurt, like a piece of rice stuck in my throat.
Once home, I burrowed in my mother's lap, her smoldering voice surrounding me:
*Never apologize when you have done nothing wrong. God himself can come down
to Earth demanding an apology, and you must look Him in the eyes and say "No."*
I return to that moment every time I pass an animal that has been permanently
stilled by a vehicle, like the used-to-be squirrel I swerved from ages ago and still
think about. I am incompatible with this world in which one can rob another
of motion. I drove by for days, watching as the squirrel became less and less and
more and more remains until it vanished one day without a trace. I kept driving.
Days after the first time I apologized without fault, I brought home an injured
bird, tearfully watched it fly away when healed. I want so desperately to be good.

II.

Though I am unfazed by the sight of blood and have no problem staring
down the barrel of a needle, I hate getting blood drawn. My veins are what
nurses call "a difficult stick" so I am invariably pricked at least twice before
the blood starts flowing out of me. I enjoy that part, watching the redness
leave my body. This I am almost ashamed of, what it takes to see that I am
alive. I often bruise afterward but I don't mind those much, sickly purple
reminders that I am perishable. What I can't stand are the apologies, palpable
concern that I will pass out from their search for the vein that yields a proper
rush. I can't fault the nurses. How could they gauge that I am ill-equipped
for those who tiptoe around their taking? I have only known the relentless
beating of ocean waves against rock. It's my birthright. Once, my mother
and I stood blanketed by the silence of constellations punctured constantly
by crashing waves, the water a gaping mouth before us. She said, breezily:
It's a wonder, isn't it, that we don't all just walk right in? Get swallowed up?

III.

I didn't travel much growing up, couldn't afford it or the demands
of state lines and TSA. On my first flight disentangled from Spirit
Airlines, I hated the first-class passengers and their absolute audacity
to dress like shit. My mother taught me that my body was all I had
so I'd better honor it with adornment. Without a doubt, my favorite
smell in the entire world is that of my own perfume. So what? That's
what happens when a child learns that many lives must eventually
fit in the void of a suitcase. This poem wasn't about you and now it is.
When we finally meet again in the sleet, I'll ask: *"How did you get here?"*
You'll laugh like always: *"I walked. It was so stupid."* It doesn't matter
how long we take. For half of my life I wanted to die. That's easy to say
now. Tonight a perfect stranger gifted me, tears welling up in her eyes,
hand on my shoulder, the exact words I needed to hear ten years ago.
I know to listen: *"Be very good to yourself. Be very good to yourself."*

CLAUDIA ROJAS

My poetry is a marker in my journey of self. I am grateful for the expansiveness of a blank page each time I start writing and give language to my past and current experiences. My legal documents contributed to my immigrant identity formation in my late teens and early twenties, when I gained legal language about myself.

I grew up unaware that my residence in the U.S. was conditional; I was subject to removal at any time, but I was also protected from deportation because my country of origin is designated with Temporary Protected Status (TPS). That I lacked permanent residence, by legal definitions, in a country where I've lived more years than any other country confuses me as much as it confuses folks who have only heard of Deferred Action for Childhood Arrivals (DACA) or who have never heard of work permits. Through poetry, I make sense of the nonsense of politics.

Over the years, particularly through community dialogue and through therapy, I've learned that the difficult circumstances I encounter due to TPS are the temporary in my life. The permanent in my life is how I think and speak about myself, how much I praise my life/living by my own terms. My poems capture the language I once had for my life, yet they are not a definite or final verdict on my life.

Temporary Protected Status

is another way of saying I have had a temporary home. I have borrowed someone's life. One decade, two decades of a permanent address in the U.S. add up to a contradiction. My living costs a paycheck, necessary fees paid to Citizenship and Immigration Services and the Internal Revenue Service. I'm always due a visit to the Department of Motor Vehicles, where my documents talk terms or talk nonsense. I frequent the Human Resources Department, where my documents talk terms or talk nonsense. I hardly ever find the Office of Student Financial Aid, where my documents talk terms or talk nonsense or talk me into another student office.

What is the difference between temporary and permanent?

A dying distance:

El Salvador.

At sixteen, I was college-bound. I could not wait. For a field of wildflowers in a New England town, for a roommate wide-eyed in the snow, for a tuition bill unaccounted for in my imagination. I only had to find new words. Not citizen, not permanent resident, not undocumented. An error in the system, a perennial crisis in the United States. I would germinate beneath a rock.

What is the difference between detention and deportation?

A temporary home:

a cell, a spell to shake.

Every year, another year passes. I am the exceptional, a performance of life. Du Bois lives in my unsleeping present: *How does it feel to be a problem?* I don't sleep enough. My face is a foreign word. Untranslated, I am a brown skin, a large continent.

CITIZEN: ARE YOU A GOAL GETTER?

Accomplish that checklist in our comfort state. Don't be a talking point, be an action point. Make your vision, your 10 year plan a REALiTY!

Quit wasting time crashing into narratives

finally, enjoy the refreshing breath of navigating
dead ends.

 -

Were you born in the U.S.? Can you claim citizenship through parentage?
If yes, *Congratulations!** Present this coupon at the cash register. If redeeming online, use code 4U$A. If no, follow our directions:

1: Are you ready for your life to change? If yes, proceed to 2.

2a: You can acquire citizenship through naturalization. Are you a permanent resident? If yes, proceed to 3. If no, proceed to 2b.
2b: Please try again when you acquire an exuberant permanent resident card. For a consolation prize, proceed to 8b.

3a: If a lawyer, employer, or U.S. citizen is on your side, go to 4. If not, go to 3b.

3b: Find someone who is on your side and proceed to 4. If unsure about trusting this person, proceed to 5.

4a: Collect your permanent resident card, a marriage certificate (if applicable), military/naval service forms (if applicable), and two selfies appropriate for a passport (international applicants). Then proceed to 6. If these forms are missing proceed to 4b.

4b: Replace the items and pay the glamorous fees. Proceed to 6.

5: They're probably reliable, trust them. Don't you want to move on to the next step? If yes, proceed to 4. Don't waste time; this special offer won't last for long.

6: Complete Form N-400. Tell no lies. Proceed to 7.

7: Pay Form N-400 fees, $640 application fee and $85 biometric fee. This fee is subject to change. If able to make a payment, proceed to 8. If unable to make payment, go to 7b.

7b: Figure it out. Once you do, proceed to 8.

8a: Study for your citizenship interview and tests. Exceptions and accommodations may be available to you. A USCIS officer will determine if you pass the English language test and civics test. Do not fail these tests. Attend your citizenship ceremony and pledge allegiance. *Congratulations*, you will then be a U.S. citizen. Enjoy your citizenship certificate!*

8b: We'll let you in on a secret . . . there are millions like you! Narratives aren't dead ends, just where the story ended or the last thing you were told. Respira.

*We can't guarantee citizenship is life changing. There is a higher chance of being treated like you're a human, but risk of discrimination, abuse, and death are probable in this country. The U.S. has two unexceptionally mediocre political parties. Voting in elections can sometimes protect you. Most people who do not experience their citizenship fully include persons with dark skin, disabilities, accents, breasts, criminal records, or bank loans. Dissatisfaction with citizenship is linked to, but not limited to, your race, language, gender, religion, sexual orientation, and gender identification. If citizenship raises suicidal thoughts or actions, call your doctor right away. If you experience sudden pain, mood changes, grouchiness, panic attacks, or other discomforting states related to your citizenship condition, talk with your local and state officials and neighbors. Seek justice immediately.

Translating

As a girl, I translated for my mother.
It was a miracle to further
the words. It was like my non-English,
the things I knew of Spanish
were a vocabulary dragged to the altar,
and I, at odd angles, prayed aloud.

¿Cómo se dice . . . ? I murmur aloud.
Es decir . . . I want to give my mother
a direct translation, but it's altered,
switched up to clarify further.
I pick apart, uncover accounts in Spanish
mixed with her understanding of English.

Translating for my mother is English
and Spanish valen por dos. My literacy is loud
when my family learns best by speaking Spanish.
The guests, my aunt, my mother
ask for me; I know it's not a step further
from asking to "read this" en voz alta.

Traducir means my hands are an altar.
He says: "These papers are in English."
I anticipate it: "What does it say?" My father
is at the door for a favor. I allow
the ask of the daughter he didn't mother.
Literacy doesn't hold grudges. It speaks Spanish.

Bilingual. They ask me to translate into Spanish,
push forms in my hand: offerings at an altar.

Is it unkind to hide from guests, to tell Mom
I'm going to pretend my English
isn't home? This English isn't allowed
a holiday. I don't want to interpret this further.

Living with Spanish can ache, like having a father
but not claiming each other. It's telling the Spanish
in you to speak more. Asking your Spanish aloud,
¿Cómo se pronuncia? in what ways do I alter
my tongue around this word that isn't English?
Sacrifice: *n.* pronounced
Span-ish used to be my first
lan-guage, my tongue's mo-ther.

LEÓN SALVATIERRA

"Rambo in Guatemala, 1988" belongs to a series of prose poems in my second book manuscript, *In the Land of Giants*, which uses memory to explore the displacement of the Central American migrants. Much like rivers, dreams, or visions, memory is a metaphor for continual change. Yet, unlike them, memory, always set in the past, has a narrative-driven force that finds its most natural ambient in the prose poem. My poems create a double movement between the north and the south. While migrants physically move north, their consciousness constantly pushes them south to the place of origin, where they once felt whole. Then, migration happened; and like a weapon of war, it disintegrated them into bits, carrying them away from their original selves forever. The loss of identity seems like an insurmountable obstacle. At his most vulnerable moment, the fictional speaker in the poem sees his shirtless reflection in the mirror and, almost as a survival instinct, reimagines himself becoming the other, "a trained muscular soldier like Rambo," foreshadowing the battles to come as he and other migrants advance north.

Rambo in Guatemala, 1988

In Nicaragua, we couldn't watch films produced in the U.S. because of the economic blockade. The night before our journey to the north, a few of us, including Xochitl, Luz, and Luis, decided to go to the movie theater to watch *Rambo III*. I had never watched a Rambo movie before. We all liked the movie, especially me. The war scenes were different from the scenes of war I had witnessed as a child. In the film they seemed more real. At that time, I didn't know that Rambo was a "cinematic representation of the Cold War," which wasn't an issue because I didn't know what the Cold War meant. Much later, in college, I concluded that for us, this had been the Third World War: the chess game that nuclear powers played for the most part in the Third World. That night, before going to bed, I stood shirtless in front of the mirror and fancied myself a trained, muscular soldier like Rambo. The following morning, I sat next to Xochitl on the bus, observing the jungle on our way to the Guatemala-Mexico border. I told her about my wish of becoming a soldier like Rambo. She smiled and said she would feel protected, especially when facing the upcoming dangers of Mexico. The coyote had warned us that we could be kidnapped, tortured, and even killed.

JIMIN SEO

I don't believe in poetry. Or maybe more honestly, poetry gives itself to me in equal parts disguise and truth. Which is to say I am the problem of my own poetry. That I can fit inside an anthology of undocumented poetics is to say, I am cornered into a rough donkey who receives—the grace of others refined into a multiplicity tool to build, cut, hammer, wedge out, make an interior palace richer than the world I live in. So many of us here, out there, have done this. If I cut a deer into the paper field of poetry, it must menace me as much as it menaces the world. If my language fails the world I live in, I must mend me and mend the world it blooms and dies in. Poetics, for me, is labor, nothing more and nothing less than that. It asks me to hammer more precisely, build more richly, that I may disguise and reveal myself fully, as much as the occasions allow.

Richard, I have lost my language more times than I
can count. A deer comes herding past my bedtime
and tears the least fragrant buds from my garden.
If only all terrible things happen in our sleep when
nearest to death or birth before the canal of dreams
winks and the biology of wakefulness tells me revive!
revive! and I walk into the manicured lawn and all heads
are lopped clean and carried off in the acid sack of a thief,
the remainder the vibrant lush of slender leaves and sorrow,
what is the name of the giant you've become in the language I gave up,
the remnant sap rimming my mouth I shout 어두워진 사슴! 잊어버린 심장!

Richard Translates

My friend, another giant of the world sleeps
for good. I'm asked to tug his tongue loose
a second time to revive him in a language
his own mother thought, *hardly vital*. As if
I could match that colossal trial between
maman and *la petite bête*. Latch him to a new
country. Wet my fingers in his mouth.
Drag his spittle up my throat, the unhinged
mandible, the soft plush of my own lukewarm
innards knowing my penning cuts him even
after his death. So why is it like leaving
a room after a disappointing night of sex,
my native tongue a sore point revised
as the last country he can never find relief.
Isn't learning a new language just a new way
of saying the world we live in isn't enough?
So why pry this giant's mouth open and
force my spit into his? Will his final rasp
burst in the air so I can convince the world
I was never good enough to bet his life on?

예전처럼 돌아오지 못하는 혀

밤 속에 떫은 향을 뜯어먹는 사슴처럼

왜 재수 없는 일들은 잠 안에서 못 지내고

죽든 살든 눈을 뜨기 전에

이몸뚱이가 깨어나라! 꿈에서

깨어나라! 하며 다듬어진 마당을 찾으며

짤라진 머리는 도둑맞고

남은 것은 새파란 몸 같은 실망밖에 안되고

배신 맞은 혀가 알던 도깨비 같은 이름이 뭐였을까

진물 입에 바르고 deer of the night! Garbage heart!

Pastoral

You wanted me to tell you something about my life.
That I was carried to pay off a debt, two hundred
steps up an unremarkable hill my mother in 서울
defeated with the strength of a beggar's bowl, no
breastplate, a generous horse, a king-blessed épée.

A city you would recognize by ear in translation
or if I preach on the fickleness of the soul. How I
was knighted my name as a foal without a sex
by a father who chartered a flight in '81 to 미국,
beautiful land, married eyes blue and distant

as the Pacific. That I was blessed two good years
with my mother, conferred a boy by my hanging
anatomy, until she was called on to be a good wife
and chartered a flight into the afterlife or at least
what felt like its economy, distant from her own 몸

Reader, I've sold you my story. I am what you think
wrongly, half beast, half boy, too weak to carry
your pastoral flag, your mule-ride, cash strapped
belly-side. You ride and whip me into starlight. Rightly,
no time is enough time 잡아도 잡아도 지나가는 시간

STUTI SHARMA

Each time I try to write a poem that is political in this moment, I cringe and close the document and work on an organizing project. I started out as a great-on-paper 4.0 GPA DACA recipient. Then the shadow that we have all lived in caught up to me. That shadow taught me that I must fight for the liberation not just of myself but for all twelve million of us. For all oppressed people. For land back. I channel my grief and rage into my work. But most importantly, I channel joy into my work.

This is not as readily received by the American public, because the invincibility of the joy of the wretched of the earth, as Fanon terms oppressed people, is not within the capitalist imagination. I don't believe in telling a representative I am worth work authorization, "legalization," because of my poems. I believe in tapping into collective power to free us. I believe in wheatpasting. I believe in our strength and audacity to create home in the face of instability. I also, above all, am a poet from Chicago, the city that has given me wings when I often felt trapped.

Where Does Your Joy Live?

joy | PANIC | joy | RELIEF | joy

DUJIE TAHAT

I bristle at being called anything I don't ask to be called. Substitute teachers were the worst. So were middle school boys. My poet friends call me a Formalist and I pupa. Cramp. Harden—James: *I am not a system player, I am the system.* The things we are called or call ourselves—like poetic forms—are the permission structures for our own being. I remain skeptical. Language is (at minimum) a quick, immediate transaction and (at most) my purchase in the longest-running exchange in human history. I obsess over the extremes. Poetry places language in tradition—even if to reject it. For now, that means I am writing ghazals. I've always been drawn to ghazals—at first, for the way they mirrored my favorite rap verses:

- the way the rhyme, usually repetition, fuels an unfolding of endless meanings
- the lack of narrative fidelity (a reprieve for my associative brain chemistry)
- the isolated units—couplets or bars—creating the setup and the punch line, and
- the final flex, the flourish, the sign-off, the tagging the wall on the way out the door

The ghazal, then, became to me, simultaneously, the least and most American form—a distinctly All-American experience. I am an irreverent maximalist raised during an irreverent maximalist decade by an irreverent maximalist nation. I am always looking for a shining promontory to leap from (a noiseless, patient spider). Form is history, a constraint for that kind of associative velocity. If all form is framed by absence, the ghazal, in particular, calls in the interruption, invites the improvisational juxtaposition. Occupying the occupier nation, I desire for the improvisational leaps to be on my terms. When I think of Agha Shahid Ali reading his ghazals, I recall not the perfectly cut universe-gems of his couplets but the jokes he cracks between, the barbs, the laughter. Form requires play. Play requires presence. So repetition as devotion. So a counterweight to the hurtling restlessness that characterizes the conditions of our place and time. So my ghazals, as my upbringing, are All-American. To the purist (apologies, Uncle Shahid), I blaspheme. I am careening, not reckless. Drink, Dujanaht. Swallow whole.

On Confession

Subjects who accurately counted the passes in a basketball game
were visibly annoyed upon learning they'd missed the gorilla suit
cartwheeling on the baseline, distracting from the difference between
pre-verbal and post-language (branchbranchbranchbranchbranchbranch),
the tree red flares, a matter of lighting, slips through the before of what
was said and the desire to never say it again, a vanishing, a returning to
the land for the migrant begs the questions: which, how, and why,
for starters, what was mine the longest was stolen last week—a red
Mizuno sports bag I've had since I was five; I'm disappearing—
my impulse to fade is a bat, at night, divebombing toward the red fruit
of the garden nested in the orchards my great-grandmother came to
by marrying a man I never met who leased a plot from the Yakama
Nation, not subject to state law barring land ownership by non-citizens,
Filipino and Japanese immigrants cleared sagebrush before being
recruited for the war or interned, and, knowing this, my desire remains
to disappear, still, my whole life I've been left to my devices, here's I—
loaded with God, ecstatic, erotic, pooled in a spoonful of light,
seeming, for the time it takes to finish, less vain, a bankless Narcissus—
responsible for a failed marriage, many crying kids, a beloved repeatedly
elbowed out of sight, restored, and again, so, here, I have to say: I am not
my father, and if I end up alone, it will be for different reasons—not even
alone, his house brims—as I turn the lock on my empty apartment, staying
with my lover for a long weekend, looking at what I don't like, I call it
an archive, and if my back hurts in the morning, it's because of how I slept.

All-American Ghazal

Ordering kebab is to make a beautiful thing out of language,
knowing, too, to make another thing, I have no other language.

Before I asked my Arab uncle the word, in English, for this bite
or that, I'd already forgotten prosody's meaning. My language

is at best, borrowed, but that which is borrowed is a blue bully's
beating burrowing its way into memory. At open house, I hid

my father, whose accent embarrassed a younger me. *Please, Baba.*
Performance bleases papa best, and my vowels have been languid

since arriving to this country. Like every lover I've ever licked—
my father knows I shape my bowlegged mouth in the language

of another's pleasure. I'll lisp, twang, twirl a lazy gerund if
the body before me shows first how it's done. Language is

a hallway of mirrors, after all. In a plea: put it in my mouth,
watch my ugly tongue make you beautiful. Anguish?

Who said anything about misery. I know my place between
the space of open throat and song. To break language

leads me to write another and another and it's a list of
catastrophes that shows you my fluency in *your* language,

but I am whistling along, absent-mindedly, reminding me:
consonants are closure, all fumbling lips and teeth—an absence.

Having daily pledged an allegiance I regret, lent breath to a nation
that spits into an already wet O, Dujie still, dripping American poems.

All-American Ghazal

If I lie in bed long enough, after waking, I'll become sad.
The trees outside my window become a symbol of my sadness.

From this angle, the spider looks like it's floating
its way toward me. The leaves shiver, and the cords, sad

with light, trap the mind's wandering. A frog rabbits
away. I let my lover leave in silence; I so love pop songs

for the way they dramatize all the little things I let
get to me about the human I love. She says, "Sure,"

when I ask what she wants for dinner. I respond "Who?"
when she asks if I think "We'll win." Once again, I'm sad

on the radio. It's a week, or two, before Election Day.
There's so much talk about Canada and making bad

plans. The disenfranchised go nowhere. God stops all laughter
yet the rain pitter-patters on a tin roof. It's not that slab

of divine sibilance, a semblance or slice of some devotion
I'm after—just the certainty of another unforgivably sad

morning, anvil-heavy, green as money made long by longing.
My ass is broke is where I should've started and what I have

I happily owe the government. An undercover detective
at my door and, today, he wasn't looking for A098162032.

ELMO TUMBOKON

At a reading, an esteemed writer tells the young girl sitting behind me that she's an archivist. *Never mind what your parents will think of unearthing family skeletons on the page. If you don't write it, who will? Look! Even my parents are here tonight! If I can do it, so can you! It's an artist's duty to document and disseminate.* The crowd, moved.

Art comes in waves. Figurative art evolves into Realism. Realism is replaced by Abstraction. Today, it seems that Abstraction is replaced by Representation: this good faith desire for everyone to be represented, especially those who have not been represented before. We're on a quest for the total documentation of everything, where everyone's face is on every screen. Artists are no longer artists, they're archivists.

But what good is this visibility politics to the undocumented artist? To confess my being is to risk my safety. I do not want to be visible. I just want to be left alone. What goes on in my archive is not for public viewing. Only a cop would be so interested in skeletons.

It's exactly this friction—the competing impulses toward making my being legible but not visible, open but not vulnerable—that I find generative. What happens when we look instead at what created the archive ("before the archive, history")? What happens when we fill the archive with our joint imagination and sentiment ("the dog")? Is this not proof that a life happened here?

before the archive, history

After Dafne DiFazio

theory: the history of literature is a history of war.
the boys come home and write their short stories

> about who gets killed and who doesn't,
> about innocence and what's left of it.

the boys write about what's left on the field.
the boys write about what they brought back.

> about the things they carried.
> theory: the boys write poems.

they write too many poems
about their bodies made unrecognizable

> after bombing a country until it was unrecognizable.
> theory: the boys come home and suddenly they're men.

war is a gender after all. war is a performance.
war is such a drag. coming to the stage:

> a boy wears the spoils of yesterday to the pulitzer.
> it takes a killing to make history like this.

here's what they don't tell you about gender: something has to be lost.
and they build libraries for those that gained everything

> the boys shot all the water buffalos in Vietnam.

the boys shot all the water buffalos in the Philippines.

the metaphor goes: you can tell a true war story
by killing a water buffalo. it can't speak after all.

the gun took the words out of its mouth.
the hills, witnessing all of this, dare not to speak

in fear another bomb may land into its song.
theory: this is what we lost.

the dog

behind the walls, the dog sits waiting
for food. it is the only thing in there.
a circumference of about 80 miles,
mortar & marble, surrounding hunger.
the dog eats—

that's not important.
you know what dogs eat.

the metaphor is not about the dog.
the metaphor is not that we contain
what we already know or that we
respond unevenly to what we fear.
i just wanted to sit with you for a while
& hold still a living thing long enough
for abstraction. think the same things.
share the same imagination for however
brief.

the dog has a collar.
the dog doesn't have a collar.
the dog belongs to someone or no one
or just looks good in a collar.

i'm so lonely. lonely enough to invent
dogs & walls. companions & defenses.
and a reader who will listen. thank you.
thank you for stopping by.

JESÚS I. VALLES

At the time of writing this statement, more than thirty thousand Palestinians have been killed by the Israeli government with the assistance of US military aid. Four days have passed since "the Flour Massacre," a horrifying day when over 760 Palestinians were injured and 112 were killed by Israeli tanks and snipers while waiting for aid in northern Gaza. This morning, on my phone, I watched a Palestinian child mourn her mother, and I read about amputations performed on other children without anesthesia. Later, I saw the photo of a robotic dog paired with the promise that Gaza will become a testing ground for military robots, the same robots promised by Customs and Border Patrol at the US/Mexico border. I am watching a genocide unfold from my palm, the architecture of this nation and our global present and domestic futures laid bare in Palestine, and I feel every word I have ever written curdle.

At this moment, I am experiencing such a tremendous distance from the person who wrote the poems you are reading in this anthology. I feel increasingly these days like the seduction of the lyric has made me a toothless confection in the belly of the beast. I am also grateful that Undocupoets gave me the space to write poems for a time, to document the small life I lived in these stanzas. I ask that as you read these poems, you think of all the ways the struggle for Palestinian liberation is always entwined with migrant justice here. I wish I had made this steadfast connection much, much sooner.

*And one day, after being called a plague, an
animal, an alien, this thing happened*

It began with the legs.

First, the bones curved, then folded into bows. The kneecaps were springs now.
The calf muscles unfurled themselves into strings. There were pockets of air
now where our heels once had bone. We laughed at their walls now, their chain-
link fences, with our new legs. Our legs laughed.

Or they sang. It was curious. Our new legs made a thing like laughing and sing-
ing. The strings, mid-leap, would catch the air, pluck themselves into birdsong
or cicadas praying before they bloom or our grandmothers quietly blessing the
land and cursing the men who took it.

There were fields of us now, gathered and from everywhere, everyone, the same
song, cry, and curse. Everything called border shattered, checkpoints shook,
then collapsed, and everything uniformed and armed was naked, still, and si-
lent enough to listen to this song; this end.

And we remembered the thing abuelita had always said about the end of the
world. That the world ends every day for someone. That every world ends.
There, that summer full of corn, rain, and witchcraft, where we sat and watched
the grasshoppers with her, and learned how to die best.

And when this world ended, and nothing needed a passport or a birth certifi-
cate, our shoulders broke open. The blades splintered into shards, plumes, can-
opies, opaque, translucent, and just like nighttime and oil-slick. We were every
bit of glory and wildness. God, we grew wings.

Algo asi como chapulines.

A Dream of Ganymede: Oil on Canvas: Ricardo Partida: 2019

Zeus descends, an eagled, hungry fucking,
dick taloned for soft meat, a just-stewed boy,
a steward for his cup, Zeus thinks, and soon
the capture: a myth, a history of me, of taking.

Ganymede was beautiful, so his seizing was just
is the logic, so is the logic that I too was beautiful,
even if during he called me fat and meant ugly,
if he called killing every bright thing in me fucking?

Let many men tell it and lose yourself in the names:
Was it Tantalus, or Minos, or Zeus draped in flesh?
I do not know his name. I couldn't see the feathers.
Where did it happen? A hotel room in Round Rock?

Conjecture of compensation: Hermes brought horses
to Ganymede's grieving father. Tros was told his boy
was now a dazzling made of burning pinpricks
in the sky's skin; Aquarius. I wished myself burning too.

Ganymede's face was beaten into mosaics, his taking
told pulchritudinous, sentimental, more a tribute
to the way a soft thing can be ripped, like pinning
a monarch to a mattress and plucking only one wing.

To take the boy down from the stars, to unwrite
the taking, would be to stop the poem somewhere

Here!—give the pen to Ganymede, pray his fist fast, tight
Here! plunge sharp into the give of the Eagle's throat, until the feel of that man's

breath fights back against the steady hand, until the rapist dies from history, too
Here! the pen sops up his blood, his hard disappears from inside me,

O, miracle!

the pen slurps his bone and skin until he is gone and I never take a taxi to a hotel
room in Round Rock and his friend never takes his knee to my back and pins
my shoulders to the bed and Zeus never rapes the boy, so there is no precedent
in history or art for what was done to my body and later that day, instead of a
quiet bus ride home and my bleeding, there is gelato and the red letters of digital
clocks never remind of the only things I could see from the floor, in the dark,
when they were done. Here, Ganymede wrestles the Eagle before they make it
to Olympus and drives death into him.

To unwrite this would mean to kill a god
and worship nothing but my own will.
Here, let me make quick work of the fucker,
that story. Give me a pen.

Mexican Standard About a Desert

I can't claims cactus
flowers, eagle-wrecked serpent,
or any plant that heals.

What goddess of war
came to me as a boy; dumb,
summer-sweat wet child?

None. No corn god or
lake-born warrior, gold dust,
feathered beast claims me.

My world begins all
dead toenails, and cardboard sleds,
patas sucias

Coca-Cola sweet,
sunday stewed tripe, red chile,
fried-egg stink, and her–

Maquiladora,
mother deity of want,
metal plates, steam howl

smoke-tower silos,
machine, motor, and all parts
all American

She made me more than
anything the ground could gift
the desert's night sky.

HERE TO STAY

Excuse me while I
weep; mass production always
makes me die—no. Cry.

Everything I know
about the desert, I know
from bones in the sand–

Yes, the dead women's
But yes, also my mother's
walking on and on

OSWALDO VARGAS

These poems of mine hit upon aspects that burn bright among undocumented people: traveling abroad, marriage, and educational access. When social commentary and infrastructure tell me who I am and what I'm capable of due to my status, I say OK. I imagine these scenarios where I had the audacity to have a partner ("Mister") and follow whatever blossomed after ("Migrant Lover Syndrome"). In "The Scholarshipping," I tell on the scholarship essay and what it demands from a migrant writer. Anger and frustration run parallel to the imagery because I write from what I call peripheral spaces. On the margin, with windows to see through but no legal line to join. Because of that, I have to imagine that, even for a while, physics bends a little when I draft a poem (or three). Even through the elbows thrown to the reader, they will still see a speaker at the center, daydreaming of what they'll say on a mic—only to freeze up at that moment. But it's only for a moment.

Mister

I don't have the papers to travel to

the White Cliffs of Dover, but I imagine

it feels like the fog riding out at dawn.

My copper necklace

stays metallic even when misted.

I look for the statue of the local idol

who made this possible;

maybe it has time to officiate a wedding between me

and the mist that's gathered here today.

I want to be the groom it talks about the most,

especially to strangers that come from everywhere

to take pictures.

Migrant Lover Syndrome

In exchange for a green card,
I'll read your future
starting from your happy trail:

I get you to come out
and jump a few fences.

You're here,
lying back,

you're taken by my reading.

I can see where I tickle you next,
by these hands
that came such a long way to cradle.

This is another thing you can't tell your brother.

My teeth yellow with every year
I don't have papers.

The immigration agent will ask again:

have you ever been a beast?

we both answer
at the same time.

The Scholarshipping

Today I convinced strangers with money / that my migration is beautiful

In this essay / I spent my summers judging alfalfa until they sprouted

or when my coworker showed off his armpit / whichever came first

I nicknamed both of them "metropolis" / because I came home a city boy

Each strand of hair / was a skyscraper

clawing away at the roof of my mouth / so they wouldn't drown.

Anything that got stuck between my teeth / was my answer

when the new roommate asked / what reminded me of home.

VANESSA ANGÉLICA VILLARREAL

In May 2020, an internal ICE spreadsheet was made public, with the following repeated over and over, on every single entry: "Parole Denial Reason #1: Parent Does Not Wish to Separate." The agency was investigated for the unlawful detention of children in its "family" detention centers, and for coercing parents to separate from their children through parole. Under the Flores Settlement Agreement, children cannot be detained for more than twenty days in facilities not licensed to hold children (which no ICE facility is) unless they pose a flight risk, so migrant parents were presented with an impossible choice: release your children on parole to foster care, or stay together in detention.

The spreadsheet I used as the container for "table {border-collapse: collapse;}" is a copy of ICE's Excel document. There are a couple of things I was working with conceptually in this poem. The first is the violence of data—how it flattens and dehumanizes, reducing lives to values, numbers, rows, and cells. The table itself is carceral—words like "rows" and "cells" conjure the language of imprisonment, where complexity is sanitized, bodies are disappeared, and all sentences fit into boxes. And this linguistic intersection—carceral language and data—was something I wanted to thrash wildly, illogically against, alternating between flashes of animal tenderness and corrupted data. I began thinking about how this could even be done in Excel or HTML, and one day in a text conversation, a friend brought up the CSS property, "border collapse," which disappears borders around individual cells in an HTML table. And I *loved* that—finding the radical, human concept of no borders, no cells in the hyperlogical language of CSS code, how it can collapse borders and open cells.

In the United States, the word "parole" is most commonly used to mean the conditional release from prison on the promise of good behavior. It is discretionary, granted to adults who have committed crimes. But parole cannot be denied to children, because it cannot apply to children. Children cannot be held, and, therefore, cannot be paroled. If ICE's spreadsheet is meant to deny bodies through abstraction in language, then this poem listens for the body denied, the voice refusing disconnection, abstraction, disappearance.

table {border-collapse: collapse;}

Parole Denial Reason #1 (Dropdown)	Parole Denial Reason #2 (Dropdown)	Parole Denial Reason #3	Parole Denial Reason #4
Parent Does Not Wish to Separate	Flight Risk	Final Order/ Pending Removal	In America, the land is a ghost of the land
Parent Does Not Wish to Separate	Flight Risk	Final Order/ Pending Removal	In America, the land is the land of the ghost
Parent Does Not Wish to Separate	Flight Risk	Final Order/ Pending Removal	In America, the land of the ghost in the land
Parent Does Not Wish to Separate	Flight Risk	Final Order/ Pending Removal	In America, the land is the ghost
Parent Does Not Wish to Separate	Flight Risk	Final Order/ Pending Removal	In America, the ghost is the land
Parent Does Not Wish to Separate	Flight Risk	Final Order/ Pending Removal	inam
Parent Does Not Wish to Separate	Flight Risk	Final Order/ Pending Removal	er ica th e
Parent Does Not Wish to Separate	Flight Risk	Final Order/ Pending Removal	land of the
Parent Does Not Wish to Separate	Flight Risk	Final Order/ Pending Removal	[is the] [free]
Parent Does Not Wish to Separate	Flight Risk	Final Order/ Pending Removal	ghost land
Parent Does Not Wish to Separate	Flight Risk	Final Order/ Pending Removal	table {
Parent Does Not Wish to Separate	Flight Risk	USCIS/IJ Review	border-style: solid;
Parent Does Not Wish to Separate	Flight Risk	Final Order/ Pending Removal	border-style: law;
Parent Does Not Wish to Separate	Flight Risk	USCIS/IJ Review	empire's bottom line;
Parent Does Not Wish to Separate	Flight Risk	USCIS/IJ Review	gross domestic product: lifespans;
Parent Does Not Wish to Separate	Flight Risk	USCIS/IJ Review	}
Parent Does Not Wish to Separate	Flight Risk	Final Order/ Pending Removal	border-style: a timeline moving forward;

Parent Does Not Wish to Separate	Flight Risk	Final Order/ Pending Removal	from an ancient south
Parent Does Not Wish to Separate	Flight Risk	Final Order/ Pending Removal	the line itself a manufactured record
Parent Does Not Wish to Separate	Flight Risk	Final Order/ Pending Removal	manufacturing a state;
Parent Does Not Wish to Separate	Flight Risk	Final Order/ Pending Removal	dividing those who remember
Parent Does Not Wish to Separate	Flight Risk	USCIS/IJ Review	from those who don't;
Parent Does Not Wish to Separate	Flight Risk	Final Order/ Pending Removal	those who belong to the past from
Parent Does Not Wish to Separate	Flight Risk	USCIS/IJ Review	those who belong to the future
Parent Does Not Wish to Separate	Flight Risk	Final Order/ Pending Removal	{
Parent Does Not Wish to Separate	Flight Risk	Final Order/ Pending Removal	border-style: manifest;
Parent Does Not Wish to Separate	Flight Risk	Final Order/ Pending Removal	"future"=forgetting
Parent Does Not Wish to Separate	Flight Risk	Final Order/ Pending Removal	(who is entitled to a destiny?)
Parent Does Not Wish to Separate	Flight Risk	Final Order/ Pending Removal	}
Parent Does Not Wish to Separate	Flight Risk	Final Order/ Pending Removal	parent-table=td nth-child {
Parent Does Not Wish to Separate	Flight Risk	Final Order/ Pending Removal	the fates = child.value (row. cells)
Parent Does Not Wish to Separate	Flight Risk	Final Order/ Pending Removal	cell value: the wolf womb;
Parent Does Not Wish to Separate	Flight Risk	Final Order/ Pending Removal	: the timewound;
Parent Does Not Wish to Separate	Flight Risk	Final Order/ Pending Removal	: the dark pines shining back eyes;
Parent Does Not Wish to Separate	Flight Risk	Final Order/ Pending Removal	: the shineback;
Parent Does Not Wish to Separate	Flight Risk	Final Order/ Pending Removal	: the wailing woman;
Parent Does Not Wish to Separate	Flight Risk	Final Order/ Pending Removal	: the strike from a man;
Parent Does Not Wish to Separate	Flight Risk	Final Order/ Pending Removal	: the scalpel of the state;

Parent Does Not Wish to Separate	Flight Risk	Final Order/ Pending Removal	: the cut flower;
Parent Does Not Wish to Separate	Flight Risk	Final Order/ Pending Removal	: the fist in the girl;
Parent Does Not Wish to Separate	Flight Risk	Final Order/ Pending Removal	: the half-moon between nations;
Parent Does Not Wish to Separate	Flight Risk	Final Order/ Pending Removal	: the first-generation border patrol;
Parent Does Not Wish to Separate	Flight Risk	Final Order/ Pending Removal	: the drawing of a cell;
Parent Does Not Wish to Separate	Flight Risk	Final Order/ Pending Removal	: the coyote's den;
Parent Does Not Wish to Separate	Flight Risk	Final Order/ Pending Removal	: the way out;
Parent Does Not Wish to Separate	Flight Risk	Final Order/ Pending Removal	} /* Global values */
Parent Does Not Wish to Separate	Flight Risk	SOUTH TEXAS ICE PROCESSING	<input id="orphans" value=unset>
Parent Does Not Wish to Separate	Flight Risk	EL PASO SERVICE PROCESSING	orphans=5500|initial;
Parent Does Not Wish to Separate	Flight Risk	PORT ISABEL	orphans: inherit;
Parent Does Not Wish to Separate	Flight Risk	SOUTH TEXAS ICE PROCESSING	orphans: revert;
Parent Does Not Wish to Separate	Flight Risk	Final Order/ Pending Removal	child-table=nested; border-style: hidden;
Parent Does Not Wish to Separate	Flight Risk	Final Order/ Pending Removal	display: table cell;
Parent Does Not Wish to Separate	Flight Risk	Final Order/ Pending Removal	overflow: hidden;
Parent Does Not Wish to Separate	Flight Risk	Final Order/ Pending Removal	visibility: hidden;
Parent Does Not Wish to Separate	Flight Risk	Lost/Deceased	border-color: inherit;
Parent Does Not Wish to Separate	Flight Risk	Lost	(every migration is the carrying of a child
Parent Does Not Wish to Separate	Flight Risk	Lost/Does Not Exist	toward home)
Parent Does Not Wish to Separate	Flight Risk	UNKNOWN (age 4 mo.)	}
Parent Does Not Wish to Separate	Flight Risk	Lost/Missing	border-style: family photo;

Parent Does Not Wish to Separate	Flight Risk	Lost/Deceased	"mira el piojito en chanclas"
Parent Does Not Wish to Separate	Flight Risk	Final Order/ Pending Removal	screaming for his mother
Parent Does Not Wish to Separate	Flight Risk	Final Order/ Pending Removal	next to the man with the gun
Parent Does Not Wish to Separate	Flight Risk	Final Order/ Pending Removal	chyron: EXPERTS DEBATE
Parent Does Not Wish to Separate	Flight Risk	Final Order/ Pending Removal	a child's abject terror, abstracted on loop
Parent Does Not Wish to Separate	Flight Risk	Final Order/ Pending Removal	(child unnamed, no consent for photo given)
Parent Does Not Wish to Separate	Flight Risk	Final Order/ Pending Removal	sound check
Parent Does Not Wish to Separate	Flight Risk	Final Order/ Pending Removal	*back to you*

JAVIER ZAMORA

I started writing poems in 2007, a time when the word *undocumented* wasn't yet part of the American zeitgeist. Harsher words were used to refer to people like me; they still are. It's these words that made me think I could find refuge in assimilation—a survival tactic. At the peak of my assimilation I claimed not to speak Spanish, a lie I used so people wouldn't ask questions about my undocumented status. Each anti-immigrant phrase, slur I've heard over the years I've spent living in this settler-colonial state has stuck to my skin like a sticker. The act of writing has helped me pull these stickers off, helping me reclaim the parts that I thought I should hide.

When I write, I'm describing the world that we've inherited. Memory (remembering) and observation of the present are necessary in order to have the ability to dream of a better future. I hope my writing can help other immigrants feel like they can be who they are. We must never forget our roots. It's with these undying roots that we can nourish the future.

El Salvador

Salvador, if I return on a summer day, so humid my thumb
    will clean your beard of salt, and if I touch your volcanic face,

kiss your pumice breath, please don't let cops say: *he's gangster.*
    Don't let gangsters say: *he's wrong barrio.* Your barrios

stain you with pollen. Every day cops and gangsters pick at you
    with their metallic beaks, and presidents, guilty.

Dad swears he'll never return, Mom wants to see her mom,
    and in the news: black bags, more and more of us leave.

Parents say: *don't go; you have tattoos. It's the law; you don't know*
    what law means there. ¿But what do they know? We don't

have green cards. Grandparents say: *nothing happens here.*
    Cousin says: *here, it's worse. Don't come, you could be . . .*

Stupid Salvador, you see our black bags, our empty homes,
    our fear to say: *the war has never stopped,* and still you lie

and say: *I'm fine, I'm fine,* but if I don't brush Abuelita's hair,
    wash her pots and pans, I cry. Tonight, how I wish

you made it easier to love you, Salvador. Make it easier
    to never have to risk our lives.

There's a Wall ft. Merengue Legend Kinito Mendez's "Cachamba"

There's a wall (there's a wall),
there's a wall where people are tanning, Speedos, bikinis, inside of a hammock
on top of the wall near the Mexican Desert.

There's an Agent, (there's an Agent),
there's an Agent (Xicanx) running
toward the people with Speedos, bikinis,
inside of a hammock on top of the wall at the edge of the Mexican Desert.

There's a Deputy (there's a Deputy),
there's a Deputy who ordered the Agent
"¡Arrest the people! in Speedos, bikinis,
inside of a hammock on top of the wall at the edge of a river in the Mexican
    Desert."

A Commissioner, (a Commissioner),
Commissioner who said ¡No!—
Secretary who said ¡Yes!—
to the Deputy who ordered the Agent running
at the people tanning, Speedos, bikinis, inside of a hammock
on top of the wall at the edge of a river in the Mexican Desert.

There's a Secretary, (the Secretary),
Secretary who told Commissioner "I'm in charge." Commissioner who told
    Deputy "¡No!"
who told Agent "¡Arrest!"
the people tanning in Speedos, bikinis, inside of a hammock on top of the wall
at the edge of a river in the Mexican Desert.

HERE TO STAY

The President, (Ohhh *The* President),
President who said
"You're fired" to
the Secretary who said "I'm in charge," Commissioner
who told Deputy ¡No!
who sent Agent running
toward the tanners in Speedos, bikinis, inside of a hammock on top of the wall
at the edge of a river in the Mexican Desert.

¡& the wall is me! (¡Yes it's me!)
I'm wearing a Speedo (¡Yes he is!)
Inside a bikini (¡Yes he is!)
I'm not Mexican (¡No he's not!)
¡Let me tan please! (¡Let him be!)
Please let me breathe (¡Let him live!)
Fuck the B.P. (¡Yes, fuck them please!)
Asi, asi, asi mamacita asi.
Asi, asi, asi mamacita asi . . . y yá.

At the Naco, Sonora, Port of Entry
Twenty Years After Crossing the Border,
but This Time with Papers

                "Research"
I tell the Mexican border guard
who stamps my passport.
It's my first time back
in Sonora. I want to find
the exact route I took from Hermosillo
to Naco, the coyote hideout,
the albergue, to feel closer
to those who were with me
when I was nine.

"¿Where are *you* headed to?"
                "Down.
To Aconchi," I tell him.
Exactly 20 years ago the helicopter, the truck,
the detention cell . . .

I hear a teenage boy
being told he can't ask for asylum.

"There were others like him this morning."
The Mexican guard shows me his notes. "Look,
almost two hundred fifty-seven just today,
all kids. We keep a paper record."

I stay inside the Mexican immigration office,
peer through the tinted glass
the teen can't look through.

He's alone. When I crossed,
I was parentless
but there were other adults.
No one is ever really alone,
I thought before,
when I could only read news
and not *be* anywhere near
the border without papers. But,
he *is* alone. ¿How?

Someone from Grupo Beta
tells the boy there's no migrant shelter in Naco.
The closest ones: Agua Prieta,
Hermosillo, Nogales.
                    ¿Nothing?
"Nothing."
                    ¿I can't stay here?
"You can't,
¿do you need a ride?
we can give you a ride," Grupo Beta says.

A la gran puta.
Dije que no iba chillar. Estoy aquí.
Estoy allá. It does not matter. It
doesn't matter.

The teenage boy climbs into Grupo Beta's truck.
I want to help, but my feet won't move.
That was twenty years ago.

I couldn't stand in México
without being told I must
find a shelter. Without

being afraid of Mexican cops
and American B.P. agents. Since then
I've looked over my shoulder
for uniforms, always
ready to outrun, outjump,
slide under wires, hide
in the brush. Because
some of the people with me
never made it, are in this dirt,
underground, & it's perhaps why
I've never had the urge
to touch the wall's rusted
metal slats. Draw on them.
Paint them. Even for this boy
who must be hungry, thirsty,
tired of being told he can't keep walking north,
who is driven away from the border
to spend yet another night
thinking tomorrow he'll cross—
I can't even bring myself
to protest it.

ACKNOWLEDGMENTS

If there were a collective noun for gratitude, it would have to be *an anthology*.

We wish to extend our distinct appreciation and love to editor extraordinaire, Liz Velez, whose expertise, insights, and mindfulness were always the guiding voice of reason in the room, who helped in more ways than we can say here, and no doubt in countless ways that we will never know, thank you. We are grateful for Julia Kardon at HG Literary for taking a chance on a small idea half a decade ago and for the encouragement to aim big, to not buy into the narrative of scarcity, and for envisioning all that can and will come as more and more undocumented writers take the lead in their own visions. Thank you, Ella Wang and Carrie Hannigan for making sure nothing fell through the cracks. We would also like to celebrate the team at HarperCollins/Harper Perennial for the care with which they held our inspirations, stories, and many drafts when ushering this volume forward. Thank you especially to the art team for this dazzler of a cover. Belated, and yet still as enthusiastic, gratitude to all of the preceding editors and assistants who were witness to this project at the very beginning.

We owe our greatest appreciation and love to the poets found in these pages and to all who shared and answered our open call for submissions. Look at what we made together!

Esther Lin is grateful to Ludi, who roasts the best roasties; the wise women, who have been with her through thick and thin; to Nanette, who translated the language of family. And to Simone and Siena, the most beautiful "big gals" ever.

Janine Joseph gives her flowers to Matt and the kiddos. All the treats to Bartleby, who saw her through three books and was the most steadfast workspace companion and teacher of unconditional love. This collection, too, is an offering to J.

ACKNOWLEDGMENTS

Marcelo Hernandez Castillo extends his gratitude and love to his wife, Rubicela, the greatest Sagittarius. And to his son, Julian, who lost a tooth and whose tender heart, generations in the making, will live to see Palestine free.

To our parents and our friends, who shared in our joys and sorrows all these years.

And, perhaps in unusual form, we three would like to thank each other. We've never enjoyed waking up to one hundred–plus unread text messages until we worked on this book!

NOTES

1. "Alien and Sedition Acts (1798)," *Milestone Documents*, National Archives, last updated July 27, 2023, https://www.archives.gov/milestone-documents/alien-and-sedition-acts?_ga=2.220944728.1915582963.1715010014-2033996594.1715010014.

2. "Chinese Exclusion Act (1882)," *Milestone Documents*, National Archives, last updated January 17, 2023, https://www.archives.gov/milestone-documents/chinese-exclusion-act#:~:text=It%20was%20the%20first%20significant,immigrating%20to%20the%20United%20States.

3. Vargas, Jose Antonio, *Dear America: Notes of an Undocumented Citizen* (New York: HarperCollins, 2019), 205.

4. "Undoc+ Spectrum & the Undocumented Diaspora," UNDOC+, CuratorLove, accessed April 28, 2023, https://www.curatorlove.com/spectrum.

5. Harney, Stefano and Moten, Fred, *The Undercommons: Fugitive Planning and Back Study* (Wivenhoe, UK: Minor Compositions, 2013), 50, https://www.minorcompositions.info/wp-content/uploads/2013/04/undercommons-web.pdf.

6. Sharif, Solmaz, excerpt from "Free Mail" from *Look*. Copyright © 2016 by Solmaz Sharif. Used with the permission of The Permissions Company, LLC, on behalf of Graywolf Press, graywolfpress.org.

7. Lorde, Audre. *Sister Outsider: Essays and Speeches* (Berkeley: Crossing Press, 1984), 54.

CROSS-REFERENCES: A PRELIMINARY GUIDE

Birds

Hernandez Castillo, "Cenzontle"
Juegouo, "Sous-chef"
Kassim, "The Alien/nation/
  body in search of wings"
Pineda, "Feeding Finches"
Rocha, "Alignment"

Black Market

S. Hernández, "When Tío Juan Bloomed"
Lin, "Season of Cherries"
Reyes, "Illegal"
———, "Why Don't You
  Just Get Married?"
Salvatierra, "Rambo in Guatemala, 1988"

Childhood

Gutierrez, "Bad Children"
Jimenez, "Marbles"
Liu, "Six years old, my classmates and I"
Salvatierra, "Rambo in Guatemala, 1988"

Church

Garcia, "I Am Itching to
  Ruin My Reputation"
Gutierrez, "Bad Children"
Humienik, "Salt of the Earth"

Citizenship

Gray, "On Your First Trip Abroad with
  a U.S. Passport, 44 Years Old"
Hernandez Castillo, "If Found,
  Then Measured"
Joseph, "In the Ecotone"
Lin, "Citizenship"
Rojas, "CITIZEN: ARE YOU
  A GOAL GETTER?"

Class, Labor, and Money

S. Hernández, "The Last Video Store"
Kassim, "Family Stone"
Kuo, "Chinese Bodies, American Cars"
Liu, "The Story"
murriel toledo, "Taking Up
  Woodworking"
Olivarez, "Ars Poetica"
———, "Middle Class in This Mf"
Ortiz, "Fingernails"
Pineda, "Feeding Finches"
Quintana, "The poem where ants are
  immigrants and I am the U.S."
Reyes, "Undocumented Joy"
Vargas, "The Scholarshipping"

CROSS-REFERENCES: A PRELIMINARY GUIDE

Country of Origin

Asher, "Dog Poem"

Camp, "Pause Hawk Cloud Enter"

Humienik, "Salt of the Earth"

Liu, "The Story"

Mello, "Between Americas"

Pineda, "In Another Life"

Zamora, "El Salvador"

Documents, Papers, and Identification

Chen, "Judicial"

J. Dominguez, "Case #XXXX"

Gray, "Missing Document"

H. Hernandez, "ID"

Joseph, "In the Ecotone"

Kassim, "Family Stone"

Lin, "French Sentence"

luna tovar, "why undoc families keep so many papers"

Mello, "Between Americas"

Reyes, "Illegal"

Robles, "User Guide"

Rojas, "CITIZEN: ARE YOU A GOAL GETTER?"

———, "Temporary Protected Status"

Vargas, "Mister"

Villarreal, "table {border-collapse: collapse;}"

Dogs

Asher, "Dog Poem"

G. Dominguez, "All the Divorced Mexican Women I Meet Are Happy"

Mello, "Between Americas"

Tumbokon, "the dog"

Dreams

Astrid, "In the Corner of a Small World"

Chan, "Special Special"

Felipe Ozuna, "Is There Anything as Still as Sleeping Horses?"

Garcia, "A Dream, a Gale"

f. hernandez, "Dreamwalk Hunt"

Ecopoetry

Chen, "Greensickness"

f. hernandez, "Dreamwalk Hunt"

B. Martinez, "This poem sits atop a displaced chimeric volcano"

———, "Cyborg"

Y. Martinez, "Mammalian Longing"

Matuk, "Video Tryouts for an American Grammar Book"

Pineda, "The Yellow Jackets"

Quintana, "The poem where ants are immigrants and I am the U.S."

Valles, "And one day, after being called a plague, an animal, an alien, this thing happened"

Elisions and Erasures

Asher, "Venus, a Dollar"

Liu, "The Story"

Felipe Ozuna, "Elegy for the Ones Who Didn't Make It"

Olivarez, "Ars Poetica"

Family and Community

Camp, "One Hunger Could Eat Every Other"

Chan, "People Like You More Than You Know"

Gitau, "when they call me african american"

CROSS-REFERENCES: A PRELIMINARY GUIDE

machado, "mapping/s"
Robles, "User Guide"
Rocha, "Alignment"

Travel Out of the U.S.

Gray, "On Your First Trip Abroad with a U.S. Passport, 44 Years Old"
Lin, "French Sentence"
Vargas, "Mister"
Zamora, "At the Naco, Sonora, Port of Entry Twenty Years After Crossing the Border, but This Time with Papers"

Visual Poems

Echevarría, "Img. 1"
f. hernandez, "Dreamwalk Hunt"
H. Hernandez, "ID"
Olivarez, "Middle Class in This Mf"
Rojas, "CITIZEN: ARE YOU A GOAL GETTER?"
Sharma, "Where Does Your Joy Live?"
Villarreal, "table {border-collapse: collapse;}"

War

Matuk, "Video Tryouts for an American Grammar Book"
Salvatierra, "Rambo in Guatemala, 1988"
Tumbokon, "before the archive, history"

Water

A. Dominguez, "Flood Waters"
C. Hernández, "Border on My Side"
S. Hernández, "When Tío Juan Bloomed"
Kassim, "A Blind Spot, Awash"
Liu, "Night Swim at Shadow Lake"
Mello, "Trying Not to Think of My Grandmother's Grave"

CREDITS

CONTRIBUTOR BIOS

A. A. Asher is a poet practitioner who explores the complexities of Black identities conditioned through the transatlantic slave trade and the more recent twenty-first century immigration.

Mico Astrid is a Filipino/American multidisciplinary artist whose work explores diasporic identity, lived experience, and memory. Their practice centers the illumination of stark realities under oppressive states—ultimately working toward a greater collective understanding of injustices embedded within current systems. Mico was born in the Philippines, raised throughout California, and undocumented for twenty years. They now live in Seattle, Washington.

Lauren Camp serves as New Mexico Poet Laureate. Her eighth book of poems, *In Old Sky*, was published by Grand Canyon Conservancy in spring 2024. Camp is a 2023 Academy of American Poets Laureate fellow, recipient of a Dorset Prize, and finalist for the Arab American Book Award and Adrienne Rich Award. Her poems have been translated into Mandarin, Turkish, Spanish, French, and Arabic. www.laurencamp.com.

Wo Chan, who performs as the Illustrious Pearl, is a poet and drag artist. They are a winner of the Nightboat Poetry Prize and the author of *Togetherness* (2022), which won the 2023 Leslie Feinberg Award for Trans and Gender-Variant Literature. As a member of the Brooklyn-based drag/burlesque collective Switch N' Play, Wo has performed at venues, including the Whitney Museum of American Art, National Sawdust, New York Live Arts, and the Architectural Digest Expo. Find them at @theillustriouspearl.

Laurel Chen is a prison abolitionist and a migrant writer from Taiwan. They call on you to recommit yourself every day to the liberation of all peoples. From Palestine to Dzungarstan and Altishahr to Turtle Island and every colonized and occupied land: abolish prisons and end empires anywhere, everywhere, across the globe. Another world is possible.

Ayling Zulema Dominguez is a poet, mixed-media artist, and arts educator with roots in Puebla, México (Nahua), and República Dominicana. Grounded in anticolonial poetics, their writing asks who we are at our most free, exploring the subversions and imaginings needed in order to arrive there. As a child of immigrants and diaspora, Ayling believes in poetry as dutiful liberation practice, writing against colonialism and toward new worlds of community care and land returns.

Grecia Huesca Dominguez is the author of the children's book *Dear Abuelo*. Her work has appeared in *Vogue México*, *Latino Book Review,* the Latinx Project's *Intervenxions, Breakbeat Poets vol. 4: LatiNext, Hobart After Dark*, *Acentos Review*, and *Autofocus*. At the age of ten, she immigrated from Veracruz, Mexico, to the Hudson Valley, where she lived for twenty-one years. In 2021, she returned to México, where she currently resides with her daughter.

Juan Rodriguez Dominguez was born in Veracruz, Mexico. He is an undocumented, disabled writer of color who resides in Salt Lake City, Utah. He graduated with a degree in English from the University of Utah.

Kevin Serrano Echevarría is a DACAmented experimental writer and artist born in Mexicali, Mexico, and hailing from Appleton, Wisconsin. A recent MFA graduate, his work abstracts concepts of gender, sexuality, language, ethnicity, immigration, and sanity by finding commonalities and contradictions between these identities. Follow him on Twitter (@accented_i) or Instagram (@misterdecember1) for hot takes, makeup, and the occasional surreal undertaking.

José Felipe Ozuna was born in Guerrero, Mexico, and currently lives in Minneapolis, Minnesota. He is an Undocupoets fellow and a 2023–24 Mentor Series Fellow. His poems are published or forthcoming in *Poetry Online*, the *Acentos Review*, *hex*, *HAD*, and elsewhere.

Suzi F. Garcia is the author of *A Homegrown Fairytale* (Bone Bouquet, 2020). Her writing has been featured in or forthcoming from *Fence*, the *Rumpus*, and more. She is the co-publisher of Noemi Press, and co-editor of Haymarket Press's Poetry Series. She can be found at suzifgarcia.com.

Wangeci Gitau is a Kikuyu writer and artist living in Lawrence, Massachusetts. She is the author of poetry collections *there's the truth then there are other things* (2019) and *i'm not allowed to explain (only foreshadow and reminisce)* (2021). Wangeci is cofounder and prose editor at *Exposed Brick Literary Magazine* and an eighth-grade ELA teacher in her neighborhood. Support their work at gladyswangeci.com.

Jan-Henry Gray is the author of *Documents* (BOA Editions, Ltd.), selected by D. A. Powell for the A. Poulin, Jr. Poetry Prize, and the chapbook *Selected Emails* (speCt! Books). He's received fellowships from Kundiman, Undocupoets, and the Cooke Foundation. Born in the Philippines, Jan has lived in San Francisco, Seattle, Chicago, and Brooklyn. He is an assistant professor at Adelphi University in New York.

Aleyda Marisol Cervantes Gutierrez was born in San Isidro Mazatepec, Mexico. She has been awarded residencies at BANFF Centre for Arts and Creativity and Vashon Island. She is also a TEDx presenter and an advocate for immigrant communities. Her work appears in *Palabritas* and *Acentos Review*, among others. She dreams of living in Coyoacan one day.

Claudia D. Hernández was born and raised in Guatemala. She's a photographer, poet, editor, translator, and a bilingual educator residing in Los Angeles. She is the author of *Knitting the Fog*, recipient of the Louise

Meriwether First Book Prize, and editor of her photography book, *Women, Mujeres, Ixoq: Revolutionary Visions*, which received the International Latino Book Award in 2019. She is the founder of the ongoing project: www .Todaysrevolutionarywomenofcolor.com. Claudia holds an MFA in Creative Writing from Antioch University.

féi hernandez (b. 1993, Chihuahua, Mexico) is a trans, formerly undocumented immigrant. féi is a poet/prosist, cultural worker, designer/illustrator, and life doula. Descendant of the Raramuri, Pi'ma, and Cora peoples, féi is devoted to eradicating borders, deconstructing colonial impositions, and unearthing ancient codes for a safer world to ensure the continual legacy of Black and non-Black Indigenous futures. She is a 2023 Lambda Literary fellow and 2022 Tin House Scholar. féi is the author of *Hood Criatura* (Sundress Publications, 2020) and the forthcoming *(UN)DOCU MENTE* (Noemi Press, 2025). féi has been published in Poetry Foundation, Academy of American Poets' Poem-a-Day, *Autostraddle*, *PANK Magazine*, *Somewhere We Are Human*, *TransLash Media & Narrative*, and more. For more of her projects and services, visit: feihernandez.com.

Hermelinda Hernandez is a Zapoteca from Oaxaca, Mexico. She's an aspiring poeta, currently pursuing her MFA in Creative Writing at Calforina State University Fresno. She's also a graduate artist at Juan Felipe Herrera's Laureate Lab Visual Wordist Studio and has received a fellowship from Community of Writers. Her poetry has appeared in *Small Press Traffic*, *Acentos Review*, *Zone 3*, Poets.org, *Honey Literary*, the *Ana*, *Voicemail Poems*, and elsewhere.

Saúl Hernández is a queer writer from San Antonio, Texas, who was raised by undocumented parents. Saúl has an MFA in Creative Writing from the University of Texas at El Paso. His debut poetry collection, *How to Kill a Goat & Other Monsters* (University of Wisconsin Press), was published in spring 2024. He's the winner of the 2022 Pleiades Prufer Poetry Prize, judged by Joy Priest, and the 2021 Two Sylvias Press Chapbook Prize, judged by Victoria Chang.

Patrycja Humienik, daughter of Polish immigrants, is a writer and editor currently based in Madison, Wisconsin. Her first book, *We Contain Landscapes*, is forthcoming from Tin House in 2025.

Alejandro Jimenez is a nationally and internationally recognized poet from Colima, Mexico. He was featured in *Time* magazine as one of eighty Mexican artists shaping contemporary Mexican culture. His work and story are the subject of a short documentary for the PBS series *American Masters: In the Making*, which highlights emerging cultural icons. He was runner-up at the 2023 World Poetry Slam Championships. His debut poetry collection, *There Will Be Days, Brown Boy*, is forthcoming in 2024.

Joël Simeu Juegouo is an Indigenous writer from Douala, Cameroon. He is committed to a poetics of queer futurity that explores the ways we might get free. For him, always, there is love at the end.

Tobi Kassim was born in Ibadan, Nigeria, and has lived in the United States since 2003. His poems have been published in the *Volta*, the *Brooklyn Review*, Academy of American Poets' Poem-a-Day, *Zócalo Public Square*, and elsewhere. His chapbook, *Dear Sly Stone*, was published by Spiral Editions. He is an Undocupoets fellow, received a Katharine Bakeless Nason Scholarship from the Bread Loaf Writers' Conference, and works in New Haven's Public Library.

Jane Kuo is an Asian American writer who grew up in Los Angeles. Her books, *In the Beautiful Country* and *Land of Broken Promises*, are fictional stories inspired by the weekends and summers she spent working in her family's fast-food restaurant. Jane's essays have appeared in the *Los Angeles Times* and *Writer's Digest*. She is currently writing a memoir.

Born in the year of the metal goat, **Anni Liu** is the author of *Border Vista* (Persea Books), which won the Lexi Rudnitsky Prize and was a *New York Times* Best Poetry Book of 2022. She's received fellowships and residencies from Undocupoets, the Anderson Center, the *Adroit Journal*, the Civitella

Ranieri Foundation, the University of the Arts, and elsewhere. She edits prose at Graywolf Press and lives in Philadelphia.

linett luna tovar is a queer illegalized writer, performer, and facilitator based in Pomona, California, with roots in Zacatecas, México. Her practice is informed by over a decade of experience in youth empowerment, immigrant justice, and cultural organizing. She currently performs with LA Playback Theater Co. and is working on *Good Sleeper, Bad Dreamer*, a bilingual poetry collection. Contact her if you're into conjuring silliness and our innate creativity for collective Liberation (IG @linett_versostuna).

Born in Medellín, Colombia, **danilo machado** is a poet, curator, and critic living on occupied land, interested in language's potential for revealing tenderness, erasure, and relationships to power. A 2020–2021 Poetry Project Emerge-Surface-Be Fellow, their writing has been featured in Poem-a-Day, *Art in America*, *Art Papers*, *Hyperallergic*, *Inkwell*, the *Recluse*; *GenderFail*; *No, Dear*; *TAYO Literary Magazine*, among others. They are the author of the collection *This Is Your Receipt and Is Not a Ticket for Travel* (Faint Line Press, 2023) and *the chaplets wavy in its heat* and *to be elsewhere* (Ghost City Press, 2022/2023). danilo is producer of Public Programs at the Brooklyn Museum and, with Em Marie Kohl, co-organizes the queer reading, publication, and workshop series exquisites. They are working to show up with care for their communities.

Beatriz Yanes Martinez is a queer Salvadoran poet and curator raised on Long Island, New York, and currently based in Vermont. Their poetry is informed by bodies of water, oral traditions from their grandparents, speculative futurisms, and a passion for art and archives. Her work has been published in *Bodega Magazine*, *Michigan Quarterly Review*, *Acentos Review*, and *La Horchata Zine*, and she has received fellowships from the Brooklyn Poets and Community of Writers.

Yessica Martinez is a Queens, New York–based poet and community educator originally from Medellín, Colombia. A graduate of Cornell University's MFA program, she identifies as an illegalized person who currently holds Deferred Action for Childhood Arrivals (DACA) status. A recipient of the Amy Clampitt Residency, her writing has been featured in the *Los Angeles Review*, *Another Chicago Magazine*, and *Interim*. You can find more of her work at yessicamartinez.org.

Of Syrian and Peruvian heritage, **Farid Matuk** has lived in the U.S. since age six as an undocumented person, a documented resident, and as a "naturalized" citizen. He is the author of *This Is a Nice Neighborhood* and *The Real Horse*. Matuk's poems appear in *Brooklyn Rail*, the *Paris Review*, and *Poetry*, among others, and his work has been supported by a Holloway Professorship at University of California Berkeley and by a 2024 United States Artists Fellowship.

Aline Mello is the author of *More Salt Than Diamond* (Andrews McMeel, 2022). Her work has been published in anthologies and journals including *Breakbeat Poets: Latinext*, *Somewhere We Are Human*, the *New Republic*, Poets .org's Poem-a-Day, and others. She is an Undocupoets fellow and has a Creative Writing MFA from the Ohio State University.

maria carolina murriel toledo is a writer, ceramic artist, educator, journalist, and death doula based in New Orleans, and born in Lima, Peru. She navigates her experience with immigration and mental illness through essays, poetry, and sculpture. Her art practice Barro y Luna makes Legados de Luisiana, an oral history series preserving the stories of Louisiana's Latin American immigrant elders. Caro came to ceramics and death work after a decade as an immigration reporter in local and international newsrooms led her to study trauma. She cofounded and is story editor for Pizza Shark, an award-winning podcast studio working toward radical inclusivity in media.

José Olivarez is the son of Mexican immigrants and the author of two collections of poems, including, most recently, *Promises of Gold*, which was long-listed for the 2023 National Book Awards. His debut book of poems,

Citizen Illegal, was a finalist for the PEN/Jean Stein Book Award and a winner of the 2018 Chicago Review of Books Poetry Prize.

Pedro Olivarez Jr. is a pretty solid and overall very chill individual. He is not a writer by trade, but he occasionally will text some accidentally meaningful stuff to his older brother, who very much is a poet. Pedro lives in Chicago where he mostly works from home, plays *NBA 2K* (relatively well), and goes to the gym in a never-ending pursuit of swoleness, which continues to elude him.

Maria D. Duarte Ortiz is a poet, creative, and writer who received her MFA in Creative Writing from the University of California Riverside-Palm Desert. She has published poems in *Verdad Magazine* from Long Beach City College, in the anthology *The Good Grief Journal: A Journey Toward Healing*, Los Angeles Poetry Beach 2022, and *Kelp Journal*. Her personal essay "Dear America" appears in *Alta Journal* and her op-ed "As a 'Dreamer,' I'm never not afraid" appeared in the *Los Angeles Times*. A former CLI (Community Literature Initiative) alum, she is currently a poetry editor for *Kelp Journal*.

Janel Pineda is a U.S.-born Salvadoran poet, educator, and the author of *Lineage of Rain* (Haymarket Books). She has performed her poetry internationally in English and Spanish, and she is also a member of the Committee in Solidarity with the People of El Salvador (CISPES). Janel is currently pursuing a PhD at UCLA as a Paul & Daisy Soros Fellow, where her research focuses on U.S. Central American poetics and the liberatory capacities of poetry for Central American families.

Jorge Quintana is a storyteller and filmmaker from Sacramento, California, whose work explores identity, immigration, and the human experience of loss.

Recently named Santa Clara County's Poet Laureate for 2024, **Yosimar Reyes** is a nationally acclaimed poet, public speaker, and performing artist whose works have appeared in publications such as *MARIPOSAS: A Modern Anthology of Queer Latino Poetry* and *Somewhere We Are Human: Authentic*

Voices on Migration, Survival, and New Beginnings. Reyes debuted his one-man show, *Prieto*, to sold-out theaters in fall 2022 and continues to tour nationwide.

Catalina Rios's poems have been published in *Love & Other Futures*, *Anhelo Anhelo*, *Riverwise Magazine*, and more. She is a Watering Hole fellow and cofounder of Untold Stories of Liberation and Love, a poetry collective. Catalina loves visiting the Detroit River, especially during sunset.

Jorge Mena Robles was born in Guadalajara, Jalisco, and immigrated to the U.S. when he was eight years old. JMR was involved in the undocumented immigrant youth movement via the formation of the Immigrant Youth Justice League (2010) and currently works at the University of Illinois at Chicago. Outside of work, JMR enjoys biking around the city and setting up tandem hammocks with his husband (Sean) and hanging out with his cat (Lady) at home.

Leticia Priebe Rocha is the author of *In Lieu of Heartbreak, This Is Like* (Bottlecap Press, 2024). She earned her bachelor's degree from Tufts University, where she was awarded the 2020 Academy of American Poets University & College Poetry Prize. Born in São Paulo, Brazil, she immigrated to Miami, Florida, at the age of nine and currently resides in the Greater Boston area. Her work has been published in *Salamander*, *Rattle*, *Pigeon Pages*, *Protean Magazine*, and elsewhere. For more information, visit her website: leticiaprieberocha.com.

Claudia Rojas is a Salvadoran poeta who lives in northern Virginia. Claudia's educational background includes a GED, an AA in Liberal Arts, a BA in English, and an MFA in Creative Writing. Her poems are published in the *Acentos Review*, the *Northern Virginia Review*, Fairfax County Public Library's *Branch Out* magazine, and elsewhere. She has a full-length poetry manuscript under submission and consideration with publishers. To learn more, visit Claudiapoet.com.

León Salvatierra is a Nicaraguan poet who migrated to the United States at fifteen. León's poetry collection, *To the North/Al norte*, was first published in Nicaragua in 2012 and has been published in a bilingual edition by the University of Nevada Press in 2022. In 2020, he won the Juana Goergen Poetry Prize. He teaches culture and literature courses in the Chicana/o Studies Department at University of California Davis.

Jimin Seo was born in Seoul, Korea. He is the author of *OSSIA*, a winner of the Changes Book Prize, judged by Louise Glück. His poems can be found in *Action Fokus*, *The Canary*, *Annulet*, *mercury firs*, and the Bronx Museum. His most recent projects were Poems of Consumption with H. Sinno at the Barbican Centre in London and a site activation for salazarsequeromedina's Open Pavilion at the 4th Seoul Biennale of Architecture and Urbanism.

Stuti Sharma is a stand-up comic, music journalist, photographer, filmmaker, and community organizer born in Nairobi, Kenya, of Indian heritage, and raised in Chicago and the south suburbs. She is a Tin House 2023 Inaugural Reading Fellow, 2023 OpenTV Fellowship Rising Storyteller, member of the Undocumented Filmmakers Collective, and a cook. They tell the stories of their life and the tapestry of their communities through whichever medium serves the story with integrity and beauty.

Dujie Tahat is the author of three chapbooks: *Here I Am O My God*, selected for a Poetry Society of America Chapbook Fellowship; *Salat*, winner of the Tupelo Press Sunken Garden Chapbook Award and long-listed for the 2020 PEN/Voelcker Award for Poetry Collection; and *Balikbayan*, finalist for the New Michigan Press/DIAGRAM chapbook contest and the Center for Book Arts honoree. Along with Luther Hughes and Gabrielle Bates, they cohost the *Poet Salon* podcast.

Elmo Tumbokon is a writer and urbanist from Los Angeles, California, and Makati, Philippines. A recipient of fellowships from the Andrew W. Mellon Foundation and CIRCULATE, his poetry has been performed from Dodger

Stadium to Warped Tour to the Kennedy Center, as well as in collaborations with the California Endowment, Aspen Institute, Just Keep Livin' Foundation, and more. He is his mother's son.

Jesús I. Valles is a queer, Mexican writer-performer echoing Rasha Abdulhadi's call to you, dear reader, to refuse and resist the genocide of Palestinian people. "Wherever you are, whatever sand you can throw on the gears of genocide, do it now. The elimination of the Palestinian people is not inevitable. We can refuse with our every breath and action. We must." Our liberation is bound to one another. From Palestine to Mexico, may every wall crumble, may every border end.

Oswaldo Vargas is a former farmworker and a 2021 Undocupoets Fellowship recipient. His work has been anthologized in *Nepantla: An Anthology of Queer Poets of Color*, and can be found in publications like *Huizache* and *Narrative Magazine*. He lives and dreams in Sacramento, California.

Vanessa Angélica Villarreal is the author of the poetry collection *Beast Meridian* and a recipient of a 2019 Whiting Award. Her essay collection, *Magical Realism*, is forthcoming from Tiny Reparations Books, an imprint of Penguin Random House, in 2024. She is a 2021 National Endowment for the Arts fellow and lives with her son in Los Angeles, where she is a doctoral candidate at the University of Southern California.

Javier Zamora was born in El Salvador and immigrated to the United States when he was nine years old. He is the author of the *New York Times* bestselling memoir *Solito* (Hogarth, 2022) and *Unaccompanied* (Copper Canyon Press, 2017). Zamora lives in Tucson, Arizona, where he volunteers with Salvavision and the Florence Project.

ABOUT THE EDITORS

Marcelo Hernandez Castillo, Janine Joseph, and Esther Lin are the co-organizers of Undocupoets, a nonprofit literary organization that widens the literary community by advocating for poets who are currently or who were formerly undocumented in the United States. Cofounded in 2015 by Hernandez Castillo, Christopher Soto, and Javier Zamora, Undocupoets (then known as the Undocupoets Campaign) protested the immigration status–based discriminatory practices of many poetry book contests; for their work, the cofounders were awarded the Barnes & Noble Writers for Writers Award, established by *Poets & Writers*.

Marcelo Hernandez Castillo is the author of *Children of the Land* and the award-winning *Cenzontle*. He holds a BA from Sacramento State University and was the first undocumented student to graduate from the Helen Zell Writers Program at the University of Michigan. His work has appeared widely in the media, including the *New York Times, Paris Review, People* magazine, and the *PBS NewsHour*. He lives in California, where he works with incarcerated youth and teaches at the Ashland University Low-Res MFA program.

Born in the Philippines, Janine Joseph arrived in the United States at the age of eight and lived undocumented in the country for fifteen years. A poet and librettist, she is the author of *Decade of the Brain: Poems* and the prize-winning *Driving Without a License*. Her poetry, essays, and critical writings have appeared in numerous publications, including *The Nation, The Atlantic, Poem-a-Day, Orion, Poets & Writers*, and the Smithsonian's "What It Means to Be American" project, and she has created works commissioned for the Houston Grand Opera, Washington Master Chorale, and Symphony New Hampshire. A MacDowell Fellow, Paul and Daisy Soros Fellow, and a Public Voices

Fellow of the OpEd Project, Janine is an associate professor of Creative Writing at Virginia Tech. She lives in Blacksburg, Virginia.

Esther Lin was born in Rio de Janeiro, Brazil, and lived as an undocumented immigrant in the United States for twenty-one years. She is the author of *Cold Thief Place*, which won the 2023 Alice James Award, and *The Ghost Wife*, winner of the 2017 Poetry Society of America Chapbook Fellowship. Lin was a Writing Fellow at the Fine Arts Work Center in Provincetown, Massachusetts, and a Wallace Stegner Fellow at Stanford University. Her work has won a Pushcart Prize in 2024, and was featured in *Best New Poets 2022*. Currently she is a critic at large for *Poetry Northwest*. She lives in Seattle, Washington.